Personal Stori

My Unforgettable

ADRIANA CARLOS & HANNA OLIVAS

JESSICA RENFELDT   CONNIE PAGLIANITI   ELLEN FORBUS   KRISTA SOBIESKI   NIURKA COTERON
MARISSA WARREN   ANTHEA SIOW   MICHELLE ESHELMAN   SUSAN HEARTLIGHT   SONYA MCDONALD
RAFFY SGROI   KIMBERLY MIHALIK-BLACKSTONE   HELEN GAINES   CIARA LEWIS

ISBN: 978-1-964619-44-6

TABLE OF CONTENTS

INTRODUCTION

Welcome to *My Unforgettable: Personal Stories That Will Inspire You* — a heartfelt collection of true narratives that shine a light on the remarkable resilience of the human spirit. In these pages, you will find powerful accounts of transformation and courage, each one a testament to the strength we all carry within us.

Life is a tapestry woven with challenges and triumphs, and each story here captures profound lessons that emerge from even the darkest moments. These narratives remind us that within every hardship lies an opportunity for growth and the potential for greatness. They encourage us to look beyond our struggles and see the possibilities that lie ahead.

Whether you are navigating personal challenges, seeking motivation, or simply yearning for stories that uplift your spirit, this book is for you. It serves as a gentle reminder that you are not alone in your journey. Each account is an invitation to reflect on your own experiences and to embrace the path you are on, no matter how winding it may seem.

This collection is designed for readers of all ages, offering inspiration to anyone looking to cultivate resilience and hope in difficult times. The stories within these pages are not just tales of individual struggles; they are universal experiences that resonate with the core of our humanity.

As you delve into these inspiring stories, allow yourself to open your heart and mind. Let the voices within these pages remind you of the beauty of the human experience and the potential for greatness that resides in each of us. May you find the encouragement to reflect, grow, and ultimately shine brighter in your own life.

Thank you for joining us on this journey. Together, let's celebrate the unforgettable stories that inspire us all.

Adriana Luna Carlos

Founder and CEO of SHE RISES STUDIOS & FENIX TV

https://www.linkedin.com/in/adriana-luna-carlos/
https://www.facebook.com/adrianalunacarlos
https://www.instagram.com/sherisesstudios_llc/
https://www.sherisesstudios.com/
https://fenixtv.app/

Adriana Luna Carlos is an accomplished web and graphic designer, author, and mentor with a passion for helping women succeed in life and business. With over 10 years of experience in graphic and web arts, Adriana has built a reputation as an innovative leader and entrepreneur. In 2020, she co-founded She Rises Studios, a multi-digital media company and publishing house that has helped countless clients achieve their branding and marketing goals. In 2023, she co-created FENIX TV, an online streaming platform that showcases stories of people breaking barriers, shattering stereotypes, and triumphing against the odds.

As an advocate for women's success, Adriana challenges her clients and mentees to strive for nothing less than excellence. She has a deep understanding of the insecurities and challenges that women often face in the business world and provides the guidance and resources needed to overcome them. Her success as a business leader and entrepreneur has made her a sought-after mentor and speaker at events around the world.

Through her work, Adriana has demonstrated a commitment to creating opportunities for women to succeed in business and life. Her passion for innovation, leadership, and women's empowerment has made her a respected figure in the business community, and her impact will undoubtedly continue to inspire and empower women for years to come.

When Fear Became Courage

By Adriana Luna Carlos

This is one of **my unforgettable** moments, a memory that has left an indelible mark on my life. I share this story in the hope that it can help others who may be facing similar circumstances find solace and strength in knowing they are not alone. I remember the feeling of utter fear, the shakiness in my body, and the overwhelming anxiety coursing through me. Strangely, the scariest day of my life wasn't even one of the days when the abuse occurred. It was the day I decided to tell my family about the secret I had been holding onto for 10 years. The thought of finally saying out loud what had been happening to me in the home I lived in for so long was terrifying. It saddens me to think that the fear of revealing the truth felt heavier than the fear of enduring another day of my grandfather's abuse. He made me fear speaking up more than the abuse itself.

If anyone has ever been a victim of sexual abuse, they know the question we dread most: "Why didn't you speak up sooner?" If only those who ask could understand the weight of that question, how much it hurts to hear. Asking it presumes that they could understand the gravity of what we went through or, if they've been through it themselves, that they're choosing to ignore their own experience. What they don't realize is that the question unintentionally places shame on us, the victims. The truth is, we don't grow up thinking we'll have to explain why someone violated us. It's not something we automatically know how to process or cope with.

We all process trauma differently, at different rates, and on our own terms. The timing doesn't matter—what matters is that we eventually spoke up at all. The shame should never fall on the victim but on the predator. They're the ones who should be asked, "Why did you choose to affect someone's life forever?" Yet even if we received an answer to that question, it wouldn't take away the pain.

Today, I'm not writing to relive all the abuse I endured. Instead, I'm writing about what came after—the healing process and the work I still do to this day to heal. The truth is, there is no quick fix, and I'm not sure one can fully heal from something so traumatic. It's been more than 10 years since the abuse ended, and I'm still learning how to process the "why"—why did he choose to hurt me—and the "how"— how can I move past this and reclaim my life?

Before I Told My Family

The moment when I finally decided to tell my family wasn't spontaneous; I had been contemplating it for a while. A close friend had convinced me that I should speak up, but that didn't make it any easier. I vividly remember speaking to my aunt on the phone. She called me, and as we talked, she picked up on the hesitation in my voice. She kept asking me what was wrong, and I kept deflecting, saying, "Nothing's wrong. I don't even know if I want to say anything." But she knew something was off.

Her intuition was spot-on. She said, "I'm coming over to get you right away. Get your things ready and meet me outside." In that moment, I felt terrified but also somewhat relieved. Part of me knew that the moment of truth had come and the story I had been hiding might finally be over. But at the same time, I was deeply anxious about what would happen next, especially between my father and grandfather. I knew revealing the truth would break our family apart, and possibly destroy it. In a way, I wished I could have kept enduring the abuse if it meant protecting my family from this fallout. But I knew that wasn't an option. It was all or none.

As I packed my things and waited for my aunt to arrive, I felt physically sick. Fear coursed through me, and the reality of what was about to happen made me want to throw up.

My Family's Reaction

I was only 15 years old when I finally told my family about the abuse. Looking back, it was difficult for them to navigate their emotions. There were so many conflicting thoughts, and as the truth came out, I could sense the confusion in everyone's reactions. It wasn't handled in the most supportive way for someone my age, but they did the best they could. They were unsure how to proceed—some were scared, others sad, and all of them were deeply disappointed in my grandfather. They had a swirl of emotions, but they did the most important thing: they got me out of that house immediately.

While this was the best action they could have taken, it also left me feeling uncertain. There were no clear next steps, and I didn't know what the future held. To this day, there are still unresolved feelings and words left unspoken. I think we all have some level of confusion about how to process what happened, and there's a lingering sense that something is still left unfinished.

My family's reactions, as varied as they were, affected me in ways I didn't fully understand at the time. Some family members, particularly my brother and cousin, seemed to carry guilt as though they had let me down, even though it wasn't their fault. It was a strange thing to see them grappling with those feelings. And while I don't blame them— how could they have known?—I do sometimes wonder if they still look at me differently, as the girl who was "scarred" by what happened.

Even though my grandfather hid his abuse well, and I was just seen as an angry child for years, I know my family did the best they could under the circumstances.

The Shift After Telling Them

The first 15 minutes after revealing everything felt like the longest of my life. I was overwhelmed with the need to cry and throw up all at once. No words or comfort could have softened that moment. In my mind, I kept thinking, "This is it—this is the moment that has destroyed my family." At 15, everything felt like the end of the world. I felt like there was no coming back from this.

The emotional toll on my family was immense. I saw how their confusion about the situation, and their deep sadness, affected them. Their grief over what had happened to me became intertwined with their own personal pain. And even though they assured me it wasn't my fault, I couldn't help but feel like the one who broke the family apart.

The hardest part of it all was seeing the shift in my relationships. I had been close with my brother and cousin, but after the truth came out, our dynamic changed. It was as if they were grieving too, as though they had let me down by not protecting me—something they couldn't have known they needed to do.

The Healing Journey

To this day, I still haven't gone to therapy. I know that once I unlock this box, I can't put it away again. There is so much to unpack—this 10-year span of abuse, my family dynamics, and the deeper, more complicated layers that I know are tied to my healing. I want to feel ready for the emotional transformation that will come when I finally do seek professional help.

In the meantime, I've found my own ways to cope. Creativity has been my therapy. Whether it's through music, singing, sports, or watching films and documentaries, I lose myself in these outlets. I find comfort in my creative expression. It helps to ground me when the weight of my past feels too heavy.

Building Resilience and Empowerment

Every day is a challenge in building resilience and empowerment. Oddly enough, about a month after telling my family, I felt stronger than I ever had before. I thought that now I could finally start fresh, free from the abuse. But that feeling didn't last long. Over time, I realized that I had become so accustomed to the chaos of my previous life that normalcy felt foreign to me. It was as if my mind didn't know how to process the calm. I was used to surviving in a storm, and when the storm passed, I found myself lost.

In high school, I would stay late just to avoid going home. When I finally had a place to go where I felt safe, it felt strange. I wasn't used to having time, space, and freedom. That sense of disorientation stayed with me for a long time.

But through it all, I knew I had made the right decision, as hard as it was. Seeing my family hurt was one of the hardest things, but I knew exposing the truth had to be done. I didn't want my grandfather to have the chance to hurt anyone else. That realization gave me a sense of empowerment. Over time, I found solace in being an advocate for others. I made it a point to be there for those who needed someone to listen, to know they weren't alone.

Offering a Broader Perspective

My relationship with myself is always evolving. There are days when I feel strong and empowered, and there are days when I feel vulnerable and unsure. I've learned to accept that both feelings are valid. Vulnerability doesn't negate strength, and those strong days always come back.

One of the biggest lessons I've learned is that healing isn't linear. There are moments when I feel like I'm back at square one, but then I remember how far I've come. It's okay to have setbacks. Healing is an ongoing process, and each step forward is worth celebrating.

Inspiration and Hope

I don't let this story define me. It's part of my past, but it doesn't hold power over my future. Sometimes, I don't even think about it until something triggers a memory. I'm not sure if that's good or bad, or maybe it's both. But regardless, I don't see this event as a stamp on my soul. I see it as something that happened—a chapter in my life that shaped who I am, but not the chapter that defines my entire story.

Forgiving doesn't mean forgetting, and I'll never forget what happened to me. It changed the course of my life in more ways than I can explain. It influenced how I trust, how I love, and how I view the world. But it's also something that gave me strength. Strength I never knew I had, and strength I never would've found if I hadn't gone through it.

The truth is, healing isn't about erasing the pain or pretending it didn't happen. It's about learning to live with it, making peace with it, and using it as a source of power. It's about realizing that the past may shape you, but it doesn't own you. You are not your trauma. You are the person who survived it, who grew from it, and who continues to rise above it.

To anyone reading this who may be walking a similar path, I want you to know that healing is possible. It's not easy, and it's not quick, but it's possible. Every step you take—no matter how small—moves you closer to freedom. Don't rush the process, and don't let anyone tell you how you should heal. This is your journey, and only you can define it.

You are not alone. There are people who have walked this road before you, and there will be people who walk it after you. But right now, in this moment, you have the power to take the next step, no matter how uncertain it may feel. You have the strength to face your pain, to confront it, and to rise above it. You have the resilience to turn your pain into power.

This journey has taught me that true strength lies in vulnerability, and true empowerment comes from sharing our stories. By speaking up, we not only free ourselves from the burden of silence, but we also light the way for others who are struggling in the dark.

The road to healing is long, but every step is worth it. And one day, you'll look back and realize that even though the journey was hard, it led you to a place of strength, peace, and empowerment that you never thought possible.

You deserve to live a life free from the shadows of the past. You deserve joy, love, and peace. And though the past may be a part of you, it doesn't get to control your future. That's something you get to decide.

So I'll leave you with this: No matter where you are on your journey, no matter how broken or lost you may feel, know that you are stronger than you think. You have already survived the worst, and now you get to write the rest of your story. One of resilience, courage, and unshakeable strength.

Hanna Olivas

Founder and CEO of SHE RISES STUDIOS

https://www.linkedin.com/company/she-rises-studios/
https://www.facebook.com/sherisesstudios
https://www.instagram.com/sherisesstudios_llc/
www.SheRisesStudios.com

Author, Speaker, and Founder. Hanna was born and raised in Las Vegas, Nevada, and has paved her way to becoming one of the most influential women of 2022. Hanna is the co-founder of She Rises Studios and the founder of the Brave & Beautiful Blood Cancer Foundation. Her journey started in 2017 when she was first diagnosed with Multiple Myeloma, an incurable blood cancer. Now more than ever, her focus is to empower other women to become leaders because The Future is Female. She is currently traveling and speaking publicly to women to educate them on entrepreneurship, leadership, and owning the female power within.

Rise, Lead, Live Outloud

By Hanna Olivas

My Journey to Inspire the World

When I look back on my life, it feels like a novel filled with chapters of both triumph and tragedy, laughter and tears, struggle and success. Yet, if I were to give it one overarching theme, it would be that every moment, no matter how hard, is part of a much bigger purpose. And, if there's one thing I've learned, it's that you can turn your mess into your message—a message that inspires, empowers, and changes lives. I never expected my journey to be about inspiring others. I just wanted to survive, to keep pushing forward. But sometimes, life has bigger plans for you.

My story isn't the type you see wrapped up in a bow, with everything falling neatly into place. It's messy, raw, and real—just like me. And that's what makes it worth telling. Every twist and every challenge has been a stepping stone on the path to who I am today: a woman who, against all odds, is not only surviving but thriving. A woman who is determined to use her story to inspire the world. But to truly understand my journey, you need to know where it all started. I didn't come from a family of wealth or privilege. I was raised by a single mother and my grandparents, who hadn't graduated high school. They worked hard, and they loved hard. We didn't have much, but we had each other. My grandparents taught me the value of grit, of pushing through no matter how tough things got. They weren't the kind of people who believed in excuses. And while I didn't know it at the time, those lessons would become the foundation of everything I would build later in life.

From a young age, I knew that I wanted more. Not in a material sense—though let's be real, I wouldn't turn down a pair of Louboutins—but in terms of impact. I wanted to make a difference, to be someone who left a mark on the world. But, like most people, I had no idea how I was going to do that. Life felt overwhelming at times, and like everyone else, I faced my fair share of setbacks. One of the hardest challenges came when I was diagnosed with multiple myeloma. It was like being punched in the gut by life itself. I remember sitting in the doctor's office, trying to process the words, "You have cancer." It didn't feel real. I had five children to raise, a business to run, dreams to chase. How was I going to deal with this? How was I going to keep going? But here's the thing: When you've faced enough battles, you learn how to fight. I wasn't going to let this diagnosis define me. Yes, it was hard—there were days I could barely get out of bed. But through it all, I had one driving force: my family. I couldn't let my children and my grandchildren see me give up. I had to show them that no matter what life throws at you, you can rise above it. And rise, I did. Slowly, step by step, day by day. I didn't do it alone—I had an incredible support system, and I relied heavily on my faith.

There's a saying that you never know how strong you are until being strong is your only option, and that became my mantra. It wasn't easy, but I made a choice to keep going, to keep fighting, and, most importantly, to keep dreaming. That's when things really began to change for me. I realized that my story—my struggles, my successes, my scars—wasn't just for me. It was meant to be shared. I had been given this journey for a reason, and that reason was to inspire others. It wasn't about the cancer, or the businesses, or even the seven-figure success. It was about showing people, especially women, that no matter where you come from, no matter what life throws at you, you can create a life you love.

I started sharing my story more openly—through my businesses, through my speaking engagements, and eventually, through books. One of the most meaningful projects I've been a part of is the book and docu-series *InspireHER: Embracing Change and Transformation*. It's a project that's deeply personal to me, not just because I'm part of it, but because it represents the very essence of what I've learned along the way: Transformation is possible for all of us. We just have to be willing to embrace it. But let's be real—getting to that point wasn't all rainbows and sunshine. It took work, and not just the kind of work you can put into a business plan. I had to do the internal work, too. I had to confront my fears, my doubts, my insecurities. There were moments when I didn't feel good enough, moments when I questioned whether I could really make a difference. But every time I felt like giving up, I reminded myself of my "why." For me, that "why" is my family, my children, my legacy. I want them to know that no dream is too big, no obstacle too great. I want them to see that it's possible to build something incredible out of nothing. I want them to believe in themselves, just like I've learned to believe in myself.

That's why I created Unstoppable Figures, a 12-month guided financial journey designed specifically to help women step into their power and claim their rightful place in the six and seven-figure world. Because if I can do it, they can, too. My journey has also brought me to some amazing opportunities, like becoming Chief Branding Officer of She Rises Studios and FENIX TV. These platforms allow me to reach women all over the world and share my message of empowerment and possibility. Whether it's through our weekly virtual Coffee Connect Create events or through the global premiere of *The Voices of 100 Women* Docuseries, I'm constantly reminded of how much power we have when we come together.

Of course, I've had my fair share of doubters along the way. People who said I couldn't do it, people who didn't believe in my vision. But I've learned that the only opinion that really matters is your own. You have to be your own biggest cheerleader. You have to have the confidence to stand in your truth, even when it feels like the world is against you. And trust me, there will be times when it feels that way.

But those are the moments that define you. I think that's what being "Sassy, Classy, and Badassy" is all about. It's about knowing your worth, standing tall in your power, and refusing to let anyone dull your shine. It's about balancing grace with grit, elegance with fierceness. It's about being unapologetically you, no matter what. When I reflect on my journey, I realize that every struggle has been a stepping stone, every challenge a chance to grow. From growing up with little to being a mother of five to facing down a cancer diagnosis to building multiple seven-figure businesses—I've learned that life is what you make of it. And more importantly, it's what you give back. That's why my mission now is to give back in every way I can. Whether it's through mentoring other women, sharing my story on stage, or writing books that inspire others, I'm committed to leaving a legacy of empowerment. Because, at the end of the day, that's what life is all about. It's not about how much money you make or how many accolades you earn—it's about the impact you have on others. It's about how many lives you touch, how many people you inspire. And I'm not done yet. In fact, I'm just getting started.

The future holds so much more, and I'm excited to see where this journey takes me next. I'm passionate about continuing to grow She Rises Studios, expanding FENIX TV, and launching new projects like Lift Off to help even more women step into their greatness. I believe that we all have the power to create the life we want and to design a future that lights us up. And if my story can help even one person believe in themselves a little more, then I've done my job. So, here's my message to you: Don't let anything hold you back. Don't let fear, doubt, or the opinions of others stop you from chasing your dreams. You are capable of more than you know. You have a fire inside you, a power that's just waiting to be unleashed. Embrace it. Own it. And most importantly, share it with the world. Because the world needs you—your voice, your story, your magic. And if there's one thing I know for sure, it's that you are unstoppable. Just like me!

Jessica Renfeldt

Resilience Coaching by Jessica Anne
Founder, CEO and Radical Resilience Coach

https://www.linkedin.com/in/jessica-renfeldt-23476125/
https://www.facebook.com/profile.php?id=61557383218279
https://www.instagram.com/jrenfeldt/
https://mailchi.mp/c13ab7758193/unlimited-resilience

Jessica Anne founded Resilience Coaching by Jessica Anne and is set to release "Dancing in the Shower; Cultivating Radical Resilience to Live the Life You Love" in September 2024. Raised on a farm, she cherishes her roots in nature and the resilience it fostered. As a mother to Myranda, Claryssa, and Madilyn, she draws inspiration from their spirit. Surviving cancer, stroke, and a heart transplant taught her to embrace life fully. As a dog mom, fisherwoman, and avid hiker, she finds joy in adventure. Jessica guides others as a resilience coach with wit and kindness, valuing simplicity and gratitude. A master chef, her dishes nourish body and soul. Described as resilient, witty, and authentic, she faces life's challenges with grace. Guided by optimism and a thirst for adventure, Jessica believes in kindness and human connection. She is a mentor, leader, and friend, inspiring others to embrace their path with courage and grace.

Reeling in Resilience:
Healing Trauma One Cast at a Time

By Jessica Renfeldt

September 21, 2021—FREEDOM like I've never felt in my entire life! I was finally free from the walls that had surrounded me for 90 straight days, free from my impending death, and free from a body that held me captive for five long, frightening, and uncertain years, where all my control was handed over to a health care team and the universe. The warm sun hits my face and I'm both elated and scared to death to leave my medical team that kept me alive for 3 LONG months, but I'm told it's safe to go home now. As we drive off the hospital campus, I begin to cry—I'm unsure if this is anxiety or if it's excitement—as I understand it, they are the same feeling, and it's just how we perceive it. My daughter drives us home. I won't be able to drive for several months because if I were to get into an accident the force of my chest onto a steering wheel could kill me. All these things help me to understand that I'm still fragile both physically and mentally and have a lot of healing to do. We pull up to our house; the grass is dryer than I would have kept it, but my house is still standing despite being run by two teenage girls. I walk up the 11 steps to my front door, open the door, and all of the familiar smells of home, MY HOME, rush to my senses, and two little fur babies rush to greet me (I was worried they would forget me). I'm greeted with welcome home signs and balloons. Ahhh, home.

You see, in 2016, I was diagnosed with an extremely rare terminal blood illness called AL Amyloidosis, which occurs when abnormal proteins, called amyloid fibrils, build up in the heart muscle. These deposits can damage the heart, making it difficult to function normally and pump blood properly. This kicked off a life-threatening stem cell transplant and 10 months of outpatient chemo, which stopped the disease process from continuing to produce the abnormal proteins. But it didn't stop it from completely ravaging my heart before they stopped it in its tracks. Fast-forward three years, and living a life controlled by an improperly functioning heart (in end-stage heart failure), and I had a massive stroke, which should have left me unable to walk or talk the same way ever again if it wasn't for such quick intervention by my family, the emergency health care team who administered tPA, a clot-dissolving drug, and then the neurology team that fished the clot out of my brain after an ambulance ride to Intermountain Medical Center. The stroke kicked off my journey of being put on the heart transplant list—you see, my heart was so stiff and sick, it couldn't pump enough blood to keep up with my 5'8" 143-pound frame, which was causing end-stage heart failure.

First of all, WAIT, PUMP THE BREAKS, WHAT!? Secondly, I hope I still have your attention because this is where the good part comes in. After 18 months of waiting for my heart, 15 months as an outpatient, with frequent visits to the hospital for care, and then an additional 78 days as an inpatient in the Cardiac ICU, I was given the most incredible gift of my entire life: a new heart. A heart from strangers who didn't know me and who had just lost their loved one, a heart from someone who made the decision to become an organ donor[1] and saved my life. This leads us to September 9, 2021. (If you would like to read my full story, my solo book *Dancing in the Shower; Cultivating Radical Resilience to Live a Life You Love* will enter shelves at the beginning of next year

Seventy-eight days in the Cardiac ICU can be quite the mind game. I was there without my daughters (aged 24, 19, and 16 at the time). My two youngest lived at home and were fending for themselves. I missed

---

[1] (Administration, Sign Up to Become an Organ Donor, 2024)

two birthdays, several months of my youngest daughter's Junior year of high school, and the entire summer (I LOVE summer!) of 2021—I literally watched the 4th of July fireworks from my window seat—what a sad and lonely moment in time. All of this, and it was in the middle of COVID, so visitation had to be strategic; only 2 visitors per day, and I was on a floor where an overflow of COVID patients were placed, so I could hear the guttural screams from families who had lost loved ones, just down the hall. My nursing staff was incredible and often came to my room for a reprieve from the horror happening in their daily lives at that time, and I made incredible connections with most of them while I was there. I also really got to know my physicians—some I loved and some I figured out how to maneuver the relationship as best I could and then there was the cardiac rehabilitation staff that helped me stay as conditioned as possible leading up to my transplant and then worked with me post-transplant, one of whom continues to meet to climb 16 flights of stairs several times per week and last, but definitely not least…the housekeeping staff (Andrea still gives me a giant hug whenever I see her in the halls of the hospital).

You see, I made the very best of things that I could, really getting to know people, BUT that doesn't fill 16 hours in a day. I was incredibly heartbroken (figuratively and literally). I tried everything I could think of…I kept working from my hospital room until the day of the transplant. I read. I did watercolor thank you notes for people's kindness, I did the diamond painting (who even knew this was a thing?), but I also did a lot of soul searching and daydreaming. I began to ask myself, what would be exciting to do when I got out of that place? Hiking, camping, and backpacking were high on my priority list, as was world travel, but something that kept popping up in my mind was fly fishing. I, like many Gen-X'rs, watched *A River Runs Through It* (I mean, hello…Robert Redford and Brad Pitt on the big screen? YES Please!). But that movie made more than just the impression of beautiful men in the thigh-deep water of a roaring river (calm down, Jessica)—for me, I was completely drawn in by the fly fishing itself. It seemed so beautiful, magical even, and something my soul was drawn to. It was something I'd always kept in the back of my mind of something I would like to try one day. This curiosity led me to YouTube (oh, the things you can learn on YouTube), and I typed in the words "fly fishing" and found a gold mine of every kind of video, from the teaching about gear to the flies themselves, the different casting techniques and finally people actually documenting their days on a river, showing off the beautiful aquatic creatures they were able to trick into taking their imitation flies; rainbow trout, brown trout, tiger trout, brookies, and cutthroats to name a few and I was HOOKED (pun intended ☺). Many of the hospital staff noticed my curiosity about fly fishing and started sharing what they knew. Rob, for instance, brought in a collection of flies to show me and told me he would take me fishing when I got out of the hospital (Ya, right. People say a lot of things but don't actually follow through). My cardiac rehab specialist, Scott, shared several stories of fishing with his grandfather, which I loved listening to as a small child. He had also had an interest in fly fishing but hadn't ever done it. Before I even left the hospital, I ordered a new fly rod from Amazon. Using the lessons I had learned on YouTube for what weight and length, I got a Remington rod and reel beginner kit with everything I would need to get started, including the fly line, tippet, and a few flies.

So, the adventure began. On day 90 in the hospital, just 12 days after the transplant, I was released and started plotting my first adventure—which happened to be with Rob from the CICU—just days post-op. We went to a land reserve that he was a member of, and he showed me the basics—it was enough to know that this was a hobby that I would love. I was shaking badly from my new immunosuppressant medications so he would tie the flies on my tippet line and then explain why and what we were using and showed me basic casting into the small stream that ran through the property. I quickly realized that it wasn't going to be as simple as tying on a fly and casting it onto/into the water, but I was also going to need to study the water flow patterns, study the fish, understand what real bugs the fish may be eating, master several types of casts and really engross myself in my surroundings and the task at hand if I was truly going to be a good fisherwoman. PHEW, is that all!?

Eventually, I ventured out on my own, into the small canyon of Millcreek, where the only fish species there is a Bonneville Cutthroat Trout, which has a magical origin story. This fish evolved from a lineage out of the Bonneville Basin, 1.74 million years ago, and the belief is that it was the only fish in the region when my ancestors helped settle the Salt Lake City Region in the 1800s. I caught nothing the first day I went in, which I shared with my friend Scott when we were climbing stairs one day. As it turned out, Scott had also bought his fly rod, an avid fisherman already, and was also going to attempt to master the skill of fly fishing. So we wagered a bet. The first one who caught this magical fish could claim the prize of the "2022 Millcreek Massacre" (a title I was pretty proud of coining myself). So I was on a mission and went out that very afternoon. I set up my rig, just like I'd learned on YouTube, putting a small prince nymph on the line and an indicator (a fancy word that the fly-fishing world decided to name a bobber) waded in the creek and cast downstream from me, along the bank, where the water was running slower and was deeper. I let the line flow with the water, all attention on the indicator, knowing it would "indicate" a fish hitting my prince nymph, either from a slight bob or a full pull under the water line. The first cast didn't pan out, so I attempted the same cast, but adjusted it slightly to the left and closer to the bank. My cast was perfect, in my newbie mind, and it was an adequate replication of how a bug would float through the water because my indicator dropped below the water line! Exhilaration ran through my body, as I attempted to remember how to bring a fish in with a fly pole: 1. Take the slack out of the line by stripping the line; 2. Keep tension on the rod; 3. Keep the rod tip up; 4. Start reeling in the fish, but not too quickly; 5. Try not to let the fish swim under the bank, under a rock, or into the tree branch dangling in the water. So many steps to think about, but I couldn't overthink them or I'd lose my catch and the title. Somehow, my overthinking stepped aside, and my body did everything it was supposed to do, and I reeled in a beautiful Bonneville Cutthroat trout. The fish was on the small side, about 8 inches of silvery-gray with subdued hues of pink and small black spots, but it didn't take away from the beauty, thrill, and excitement I had in catching it!

As soon as I left the canyon and regained cell service, I claimed the champion title of the "2022 Millcreek Massacre" and have forever felt pride in having figured it out all on my own.

That summer, I continued to visit Millcreek but added rivers like the Provo River, Bear River, Weber River, Big Wood, and Silver Creek, each with its own story and strategies required to catch fish. As I honed my skill as a fly-fisherwoman, I had the epiphany something more incredible was happening within my soul that was even more magical than the catch itself. Having gone through the trauma of life-threatening illnesses for the previous six years left me with a lot to process that I didn't exactly have time to process at the time I was fighting for my life. Each trip left me feeling more joy, contentment, and in love with my life, so I started to ponder what it was about the act of fly fishing. It was helping me to HEAL in such a beautiful way, and I was able to uncover 7 characteristics of fly fishing that helped to heal my trauma and loss.

1. **Mindfulness, Presence, and Personal Reflection:** Fly fishing requires a deep focus on the present moment. The act of

casting, mending the line, and observing the water nurtured mindfulness, which helped me shift my attention away from the trauma and ongoing post-transplant office visits, brought me into the present moment, and created a calm I'd never experienced before.

2. **Connection to Nature:** So many studies show that spending time in nature reduces stress and improves moods. For me, fly fishing allowed me to become part of the ecosystem through the study of the water and the bugs and even becoming the bug itself in peaceful natural environments, which gave me a break from the noise of the world and allowed me to heal both physically and mentally. The feeling of being part of the forest brought incredible energy and belonging to my soul. Almost every visit to a river or lake elicited a very deep and powerful emotional response that ranged from tears of joy to a powerful knowing that I was   part of something bigger.

3. **Physical Activity:** Fly fishing involves a lot of physical movement. I have hiked miles to reach canyons and waded through thigh-high water to reach the perfect spot on the river. We all know that physical activity helps improve our mental health, even alleviating symptoms of depression and improving our physical strength. For me, finding something I love to do physically is filled with fun, adventure, and curiosity. I LOVE IT!

4. **Structured Routine:** When I became a patient for treatment of a terminal illness, I lost so much control, so finding a practice that allowed me to have a structured routine in preparing gear, selecting flies, and casting techniques brought back a much-needed sense of control and purpose that I'd lost in years of cancer treatments, stroke rehabilitation and waiting for a heart transplant. This was so grounding for me while healing from

trauma. The process of fly fishing involves a structured routine, from preparing gear to selecting flies and casting techniques. This routine provides me with a sense of control and purpose, which was particularly grounding for me while healing from trauma.

5. **Stimulation of my Senses:** Flyfishing in nature allowed me to use all my senses; the touch of the line, the sound of the water, and the smell of the forest also helped ground me and offered an escape from my memories of trauma.

6. **Social Connection:** Social connection was a big deal for me. Community was essential when I was recovering from trauma, loss, and grief. Making friends, having friendly bets, and connecting with others who also loved the sport were all social interactions that helped me to heal. I felt like I had a sense of belonging (not just being part of the heart transplant club) and reduced the feeling of isolation that I had experienced while spending months and months in hospital rooms over the course of 6 years and missing out on activities with friends and family due to the restrictions the disease had on my body.

7. **Goal Setting and Achievement:** I've always loved a good goal or competition for myself. The Utah Department of Wildlife Resources created a competition called the Utah Cutthroat Slam—the goal is to catch the four cutthroat species here in Utah: The Bonneville, The Colorado, The Bear, and The Yellowstone. Like I said, I love a good competition, and this was it! I traveled miles and miles and visited rivers and lakes, and I finally did it this year! This goal allowed me to practice my casting technique and taught me how to catch a specific type of fish. Achieving this goal helped me to have a sense of accomplishment, which counteracted the feelings of helplessness that my illness could have made me feel helpless and hopeless.

Going through my health journey taught me so much about myself, including how incredibly strong I am, but it also helped me uncover so many useful skills and strategies to cope with life's adversities going forward. For me, fly fishing was incredibly healing and encompassed most of the things that helped me move forward in life. I'm so grateful for the healing that I found and for the people and things that were part of my journey, and I've turned my passion into helping others as a Resilience Coach. I now help those struggling with loss and grief find gratitude, joy, and resilience like they never knew was possible so they, too, can lead their happiest lives ever imagined.

I know fly fishing isn't for everyone, but I share this as a parable for your own life in hopes that those who have struggled with trauma, loss, or grief will become curious and find an adventure, hobby, or practice that can bring the same peace, tranquility, and joy that fly fishing has brought to me.

Anthea Siow

Founder of Change Pathways

https://www.linkedin.com/in/anthea-siow-05873a204/
https://www.facebook.com/profile.php?id=100078376642432
https://changepathways.com.au/

My name is Anthea. I am a Social Worker with a Master's degree. After twenty years in Child Protection, Domestic Violence, and working with young people in out-of-home-care, I decided it was time to close this chapter and start a new one.

I became a social worker because of my childhood experiences. From running away from home to living on and off the streets. In order to get off the streets, I found myself in one bad relationship after another. A means to an end however it came with a price.

I was a single mum at 31, my son saved my life. I turned my life around because of him. It was the first time in my life that I was surviving not only for myself, but for a little person. My son is my pride and joy.

I now have an accomplished catering business and a cafe. After all that has happened, I can achieve anything I set my mind on doung. My world view, acceptance, and forgiveness is always a working progress.

Little One

By Anthea Siow

Complex, simple, beautifully plain, neurotically quirky, and deeply loving. This is a story about my childhood, about life growing up in a family where violence was the norm, and my dream of a life worth living… on my "Nim's Island".

The memories I most want to forget started when I was four years old. This is my story of survival and self-preservation. This is about self-discovery, resilience, strength; and stealing precious moments of childhood amidst the chaos. It is about my life after my teenage years, and many years following. The sweet and the ugly…

I was blessed with a few precious beautiful friendships along the way; but also, appreciation for all the mistakes and failures which I have been stupid and lucky enough to make. If not for them, I would not have learnt or been able to do those important lessons which ended up being the foundations that shaped and reshaped me. As painful as some lessons were, crazy even, there were many memorable hours filled with deep love and funny moments. Running away from home = survival! The hatred, guilt, and shame that I carried with me over forty years, paled in comparison to the life the world opened my eyes to, but everything comes at a cost.

I have squeezed into a life resembling a brown old, weathered leather suitcase that would not close from too much of everything crammed inside. I was a hoarder of life experiences, of big dreams. I would always throw myself into something. I took on whatever stood in front of me.

Any hope of belonging in any place or with any one person for a long duration of time would only be a longing rather than a reality. However, all I desired was to feel love unconditionally and to acquire stability like other "perfect-normal" couples and families. Looking back, I know that my want for the "perfect-normal" is just an ideation that does not exist in many families. Their façade looks like a dream but the interiors crumble, as relationships are dysfunctional on varying levels.

I questioned my life's purpose like I would, digging through my unkempt wardrobe looking for the right outfit to wear but never finding the right one. The title "Little One", came to be from a dear, and much-loved friend Kylie Nash, we worked together in a Women's refuge. Kylie calls me Little One, and I found it fitting as it tells the story of the Little One who continued to live in a grown woman's body.

The events to follow are snippets of time and space that scarred me for a very long time. There were many in between these which I won't mention here, but they are on the pages of my memoir, *Little One*.

I was born in 1969, and the youngest of six. I was raised to be seen but not heard; I was small, insignificant, and vulnerable. Regular beatings were the norm as mum, dad, and eldest brother believed was the right thing to do to ensure I grew up well adjusted, of good behavior, and did as I was told. It was never just a little smack but corporal punishment. At the age of nineteen, I realized that what I was dealt as a child, a teenager, and an adult was not unique only to me, but to many. My story is my truth, it made me who I am today. I became a Social Worker for a reason. I do not tolerate injustice; the advocate in me is my superpower.

Imagine kneeling on the concrete floor (on bottle caps) with your face pressed against the wall while pulling on both ear lobes. I cannot tell you how long, but every minute passed felt like hours. Imagine your arm broken by someone you trusted, someone who you thought would look out for you, protecting you from all the bad of the world, now imagine you were four years old. I was four when bad was very bad, and the worst was yet to come.

1973, Singapore, four years old. We all have a memory or memories that have left an imprint. With my big brother sitting opposite me on an ottoman while I sat cross-legged on the floor, he had leverage. A pencil in hand, a notebook in front, and A, B, C's on the page. "I don't want to see the indent on the next page," I tried very hard not to because I knew what would happen. A closed-fisted punch to the right side of my face. "Do it again!" Another punch, again and again, I tried, but when hot stinging tears welled up and blurred what was in front, I held that pencil tighter thinking if I did, it would make me write lighter and softer so that on the previous page behind, there were no alphabet indents. The more he punched, the hotter my face; more tears = indents = a punch. I could see into my parents' bedroom. Mum was reading the newspaper; Dad was hunched over his drafting table working on a design blueprint. "Help, please, stop him from hitting me. It hurts so bad, Daddy, help me, he is going to kill me. I am here, take me away, please, please." That was screaming in my head. His anger kept escalating. It wasn't until the next blow and my tiny head hit the polished concrete floor that Mum lowered her newspaper and called me over. She put a cold wet face towel on my face to keep the swelling down. It was the first of three motherly love I have felt in my fifty-five years. The second was an ice cream, and the third was a hug when I was 10. The end!

I remember vividly, careful not to make a sound as I turned the silver handle of the front door, I wanted to run away… But I closed it gently because who would look after me and where would I go? That was the first day of the eight years that I started planning to one day free myself. A blood vessel had burst in the whites of my eye that never left. I have it to this day... A keepsake that reminded me where I came from and why running would be the only way for me to survive.

In 1975, we arrived on Christmas Island. I was not quite six then. Dad was an Engineer and had taken a job there. Back then, it was a phosphate mine. Dad packed us all up, left on a jet plane, and left big brother behind. It was just us three sisters, mum and dad. I was safe, but not for long. My very bad, bad luck. The dread, panic, I have never forgotten that indescribable feeling in the pit of my stomach the day he arrived on the island.

Mum was having a shower; I was sitting on the floor in front of him. He sat with his back to the wall, in his right hand was Dad's large fishing knife. The kind with a wide blade, one side was serrated, and the other side was a sharp edge. His left forearm resting on his knee and with the knife in his right hand, he made long cuts into his arm, over and over. I sat there frozen, too scared to get up and leave and too scared to sit in front of him. Again, the screams in my head were going off but nobody heard, no one came, and Mum was still in the shower. He's going to cut me, watching the blood run down his arm and droplets of blood pooling on the floor. I knew at nearly six that what he was doing was not normal, and I was part of this abnormality, this very dysfunctional family. A big knife, cut flesh, blood = trauma!

1977, Griffith Avenue, Bondi, Sydney. I was eight years old. I shared the bedroom with my two sisters. Sleeping on the top bunk bed was the lesser of two evils. If I had slept on the empty bottom bunk, I would have been fair game for big brother. On the top bunk, I would scoot as close as I could to the wall. I pressed my back against it so that I could feel the cool of the wall through my pajamas. In a fetal position with my arms wrapped around my legs, and knees to my chest, buried under my doona, I would be safe. You can't see me, then I wasn't there. So stupid! When there is a perpetrator, you are never safe. Every time I smell his cologne, Aramis, I would freeze, my heart thumping, I would squeeze my eyes shut thinking if he saw I was sleeping, he would leave me alone. But he never left. I would feel his hands on my legs, then between my legs, up my legs. Then I heard my mother… Stop doing that, you are her big brother." He says as he laughs… "I'm just teasing her." I hated sleep, I hated having to go to bed. I never had a peaceful night's sleep because when he was home, I died a little with every touch.

1978, Five Dock, Sydney. My second oldest brother had finished his National Service in Singapore and came to Australia. He was at Sydney University studying Medicine. I loved him the most. He was the nice brother I adored. That soon changed when he slapped me across the face twice. To this day, I don't know what I did. Once more, the love I felt for an older brother who I thought would protect me, had hurt me. The slap wasn't what hurt, it was the betrayal and my misplaced love. I grew a distance between us after that. I withdrew and went inward.

1981, Drummoyne, Sydney. I was the first to go to bed, at 7:30 pm every night. As I was trying to fall asleep, big brother came into the room. He sat on a bed, not mine as I didn't have a bed but a straw mat on the floor a blanket, and a pillow. "Are you sleeping?" He called my name, and I cringed. He repeated, "Anthea, are you asleep?" I can hear him masturbating himself. It sickened me, the sounds of him pleasuring himself were deafening in my head. One which stayed with me for a very long time. That went on most nights, for too many years.

By the time I was fourteen, he had been through many girlfriends, all he bashed, never behind closed doors. They lived with us for a short time. When he had girlfriends, I was left alone, but as each one left, the focus came back on me. He was transient with his moods, cycling between bashings and "what we have is very special, but you can't tell anyone about this because they won't understand this special bond." BOND??? SPECIAL??? Really??? His words were crass, I knew all that was not normal, and yet, through bashings and grooming, he had me in arms reach.

"Hey, I told Mum I need your help with unpacking at my house." Oh shit, no...went through my head, what followed was insane. "I don't need you to unpack, I just told Mum that so she would agree. You mustn't tell anyone, you promise?" "Yes" was all I could say. "I want you to take photos and video me fucking Leslie, this is your sex education." There were no words for this, he took it to the next level. The family never understood why I was so head fucked growing up, no one cared enough to ask why I acted out, why I became rebellious, why I would swallow as many of Mum's Valiums…did I want to die? Yes! I never wanted anything more. I longed for it every day of my life.

> "Eyes afraid to open,
> scared of the thoughts each day,
> this life of mine has never been mine.
> I cry out for help, knowing it never comes,
> I don't want to be here another broken day."

The sex-ed day happened to be the same day he told Mum he needed my help. He wasted no time. I sat in the back seat of his car with Leslie in the front passenger seat. He chatted away as if what was about to happen was an ordinary everyday activity. It wasn't until in my thirties that I wanted answers, was she as sick as he was? Was she into it or was she also a victim of his sick manipulation and twisted game of self-gratification? I didn't know "pedophile" was even a word back then. He was a PEDOPHILE!

We pulled into his driveway; unopened boxes littered the house. To stall time, I offered to help unpack boxes, the only box I had to unpack was the one the camera/video was in. Leslie was naked and on the bed. He was naked and with a hard-on. Me, looking through the lens. What your eyes see, you cannot unsee. Don't touch me, I pushed his hands away, again and again. That day, I learnt about how a woman pleasures herself by doing things to her clitoris. I didn't know at the time, that was what it was. Leslie was into it; she didn't act like she was coerced. I leave it to your imagination because to write it in words is too filthy and the words to describe what happened that day would be too expletive. Flight, fight, or freeze… I froze.

1986, Dundas Valley, Sydney, aged seventeen. It was a Saturday; the family went out. As usual, I stayed home with a list of chores to get through. I packed what I could into garbage bags (that's what my seventeen years amounted to, garbage bags). I stole the telephone bill money; I called a cab and that was the last I saw of them until my son was born in 2000. I lived on the streets for the most part of two years. I couch surf when I could, making sure I didn't overstay. I was studying to become a nurse at university and every day, what possessions I had left with me all fitted into a locker at the Prince Alfred pool. I would shower at the pool, look as normal as I possibly could, and go to classes. I was in my first year. Living on the streets, you lose many belongings. When you put it down, walk away, come back and it is gone. I was determined to get off the streets, being hungry most days and finding a little safe nook to sleep wasn't easy. Always woke up before sunrise so no one would know the space under the stairs was my home for the night. Being homeless was temporary. Dying on the streets or succumbing to insanity was not an option. I couldn't sustain studying, so I had to defer until...

One Sunday, walking in the city a man in a bottle green suit said hello and asked if I remembered him. I said no, should I?" He said he was Brendan, my date at my year ten graduation formal, and it all came back to me. He asked me out and I said yes. There was my ticket off the streets. I stayed at his place which he shared with a single mother and her sixteen-year-old daughter, and two years later, I caught them with his penis in her mouth. I dragged him down the stairs and out the front door. Bondi Road is bustling on a Saturday afternoon, chucking him out naked was mild in comparison to what I really wanted to do. The Royal Bondi Hotel was entertained that afternoon. I didn't get away unscathed, he cracked my skull, broke my left foot, and kicked my dog... SCUM. Two things I was able to achieve by being in that relationship were getting off the streets and returning to university. Was it worth the price I paid? At 19, yes it was, but if you ask the 55-year-old me now, I will tell you that no one should ever put themselves in harm's way. There are safer ways and people are willing to help if you reach out. Had I known then, I would have asked for help... I grew up with violence, with incest, I was numb inside and unconsciously I went from one abusive relationship to another. The psychological abuse which comes hand in hand with physical abuse to me, was 100 times worse than having a broken bone, or bruises. Bones heal and bruises go, but the psychological and emotional trauma is a long-term scar that others cannot see and one I struggled with. Trusting myself and trusting others, I didn't have that privilege.

That was my life. I decided to go back and study to become a social worker,I wanted to be a child protection worker, an advocate for the homeless and for women and children in domestic and family violence which I practiced for 20 years.

09/11/2000, Royal North Shore Hospital age 31. My son Ky was born at 2:10 am. I had the most beautiful baby with golden hair, fair skin, tiny fingers and toes. I welcomed my life as a single mum. Ky was my saving grace. He changed the trajectory of my life. The love I had for my baby was one I had never felt or received up until he came into my life. Everything I was role-modelled by my mum, I abandoned. I was not going to be that to him. Loving him unconditionally, holding him, and being his mum was exactly where I wanted to be. Being a single mum was not difficult. Ky was a very good baby, and he was a great kid as the years passed. When I was studying social work, I would take him to lectures. He never cried or screamed; he made my life so easy. When he was 6, I took him to the Wayside Chapel where I worked with the homeless, people with mental illness, and those with drug/alcohol dependencies. People become homeless for many reasons

I would tell Ky, sometimes it is because they have taken too many drugs, lost their jobs, or their homes, and sometimes they have mental illness but never judge them for it because it can happen to anyone and at any time.

Ky was popular with everyone, and he was great with them too. I wanted him to see that everyone is not as fortunate, and the realities of life can be harsh, and they are human beings. Ky grew up with empathy and compassion. He would always give his pocket money to the homeless. Ky had humility, kindness, compassion, and empathy. You can't teach those things, so I knew he would never be the type of person who would hurt another person. Present day, he is a youth worker and studying social work. This mama is very proud of the man he has become. He has a beautiful partner, and I love the way they are with each other, to see them balance each other, respecting and valuing one another. I am at peace.

Big brother thought he could pick up where he left off 20 years ago. Anger flowed in my brain, hatred ate me up every day, reliving the trauma of childhood, as a young person, and as an adult. I was torn between having a family after having no family since 17 or walking away to keep myself sane. I chose to walk away on February 27, 2017, the day my father passed away. but it took me another ten years to find the right help. Thank you, Kim Hopson. You saved my life.

I walked into Kim's clinic; I couldn't make eye contact. As she sat opposite me, I said "This is my last place of call. If this doesn't work, it will be the end of me. I am giving up. I can't do this anymore." Kim said, "You must jump in with both feet and bring your imagination." The Richard Trauma Process (TRTP) modality, 1 session per week over 3 weeks, and each session being 2 hours. Kim wasted no time. As I sat there thinking, "Please, say this isn't Gestalt." She created a very safe space, I went deeper into visualizing a stage, and on that stage there he was. I had to confront him and unleash all the years of hurt, anger, and hatred. When I went back to the "I can forgive you, but I can't forget" stage, Kim would stop me and pull me back on track, back to anger, and back to the "I" statements. "I am not shit, I don't deserve to be treated like shit, I am enough, I am more than enough…" After that first session, I felt an immense shift in my thoughts. I felt oddly positive and empowered, which I never knew would be possible. That was the start of the rest of my life. I was also in a marriage where intimacy was a vacant post. I couldn't live another day of criticism, coercion, negativity, control, and abuse; he was the male version of my mother. I learnt how to move forward, and to stand up for myself, I am not at fault. Guilt, self-pity, loathing, self-destruction, anger, and hate, were no longer a noose around my neck. I knew I would make it when I thought of the pedophile, and my mum, my insides twisted and wound up so tightly no longer had a place. I went on to complete the Master of Social Work. I left my marriage and home to find my little pocket of heaven on a little island on the Pittwater in Sydney, my Nim's Island. Life is great. I am happy, I am comfortable in my own skin, I know who I am, my boundaries, and what I will and will not tolerate. When to walk away and when to stay.

"The heavy burden weighs on your soul
You will forever look behind you and wonder if anyone else knows.
I am no longer the victim, I will heal from within
I don't need to make you accountable anymore

What has passed can no longer hurt me.
As each day passes,

You are one step closer to your maker,

Your judgement day will come
I no longer need to seek justice, as I know justice will be served.
I will do it my way and live a worthy life

The shackles have fallen, I am free at last."

I have two beautiful foster children, Jessica and Ricky. To them, I am mum, to me they are my world. Ricky had come to us in 2015 with trauma at 14 months old. Our relationship had a rocky start but as he got older, he has settled into the most insightful, emotionally intelligent child I know. He is a great kid with a huge heart. My belief is that children who have experienced trauma have a great insight into their emotions. It is the role of the carers to guide them, protect them, celebrate their successes, to love and nurture them during the times when it all seems too hard. He is the most loving kid and I hope he stays this way as he gets older.

Jessica was 4 months old when she came to us. She is confident, she knows herself, what she likes and doesn't, who is good and who isn't. I love that she is strong-willed, and I hope that it will help her in the future. She is my heart. My little one didn't come with trauma as she was removed at 5 days old from the biological mum.

2023, my Nim's Island, Pittwater. I don't need a man to define me or for the sake of having one. I met this man 15 years ago. I didn't want a committed relationship after my marriage. I went in with a no-strings-attached, casual, and on-my-terms attitude but eight months later, heaven is a place on earth. He loves me for who I am, I don't need to change to fit in with him, I know what true love looks like, how it feels, and how safe I feel when I am with him. When someone truly loves you, he won't burn you, criticize, gaslight, or make you feel less like a person. A good man will not tear you down for his own gratification, when you love and value yourself, you know what you want in life… I look at this man I love, value, and appreciate, and I know deep in my heart that I worked very hard to differentiate the difference between healthy and unhealthy love. I never knew I could love someone apart from my children the way I do with him. I have never met a respectful man, who I can easily talk to, laugh with, and love unconditionally, and have the capacity to watch this unfold. For now, he is home.

"Home isn't the bricks or mortar that shelters us from the storm.
It isn't the furnishings between these walls
It isn't the silent meals between two people
It isn't the sound of doors closing
It isn't a home if it tears our world apart.
Home is the familiar scent of the one you love
It is the hand you long to hold
It is the blanket of warmth in the absence of the sun
It is the us. There is no I.
It is the promise, without needing to be spoken.
Home to me, as it will always be
In my heart where I know you'll be.
It is in your smile, your eyes, your lips
It is in your arms when you hold me.
It is in every detail of your body
Which I can trace with my eyes closed.
It is in your voice
When you laugh or tell me a story
It is in your honesty and integrity
It is knowing we're home without
Having to open the door.
A house is just a house built from bricks and mortar
But a house is a home when there's love and warmth within.
It is a space where you can just breathe,
Without being changed into someone you don't want to be.
Home is where our heart is, and trust is the shelter from the storm."

My memoir tells my story of adversity, the cost of freedom, and the journey of finding who "Little One" is. It is raw, honest, and provoking. I lost my childhood, but I grew as a woman who survived child abuse… There is nothing more empowering than putting down the past and running towards the rest of your life on your terms. My past does not define who I am, I do.

Marissa Warren

Marissa Warren
Hypnotherapist & Transformational Consultant

https://www.linkedin.com/in/marissawarren-hypnotherapist-transformationalconsultant/
https://www.facebook.com/marissa.warren.transformational
https://www.instagram.com/marissawarren_/
https://www.marissawarren.com/

Marissa is a globally renowned clinical hypnotherapist and transformational consultant working with RTT – Rapid Transformational Therapy, QHHT – Quantum Healing Hypnosis Technique, Somatic and Tantric embodiment, breathwork and sound healing. I am an international speaker and author.

Marissa embodies these modalities in her life and have used these to heal trauma, make major changes, create transformations and align to her soul's and life's purpose.

For those ready to reclaim inner freedom, break free from past limitations, step into their best life, take action, are ready to uplevel and elevate their life, want to achieve true transformations, and realign with their souls' purpose and align to their own unique authenticity and sovereignty – Marissa is the transformational consultant to help!

Leaving you feeling empowered, living from infinite inner power and potential and stepping into the life and level of success you desire. Marissa will help you tap into your inner magic and utilise your inner resources to step up and shine.

Marissa has a phenomenal ability to tap deeply into people's subconscious to help them break free from internal limitations, negative patterns and behaviours and allow them to move into living their dream life and souls purpose.

Journeying Through the Abyss of My Soul; Accessing Hidden Depths for True Inner Freedom

By Marissa Warren

"NO MORE!"
"THIS IS NOT THE LIFE I AM MEANT TO BE LIVING!"
"WHAT AM I HERE FOR?'
"WHAT IS My LIFE PURPOSE?"

This is what I was asking myself after my father died four years ago. There is nothing like death to face the mortality of life....

I looked around at my life and realised that I didn't want my next 40 years to be the same as the last 40 years had been. While I have lived a full life, with a lot of varied experiences, going through the grieving process really brought a lot to the surface that I had buried so deep down that it was long forgotten, blocked out and completely repressed.

My life has been an all-roads lead in the right direction and it wasn't until I reached a certain point in my life, that I could look back over all of the events that had occurred and see how interconnected everything was. If it wasn't for what had happened in my life, I wouldn't be where I am today.

The journey through life hasn't been easy. I've had to navigate my father being sick with cancer, multiple times, for the majority of my life, which led to me having to be hyper-independent due to absent parents – not through neglect but through necessity. My mum worked multiple jobs to support the family and my father was sick. At the age of 8 with my father's first cancer diagnosis, he was told that he would have 6 months to 1 year to live. My father was a stubborn man and went on to live for another 32 years and was able to move through not only 1 but 2 major cancers before the 3rd was the final one that he was not strong enough to battle through at 72 years old. All of this gave me a warped sense of the reality of life and death. I never feared dying, I always feared not living. I never wanted to get to the end of my life with regrets and feel that I missed out on any experiences along the way. Not all experiences were great… There have been toxic and abusive relationships, bad and reckless lifestyle choices, fertility challenges and many moments I think I could have made a different choice. I wouldn't change these experiences as they make up the tapestry of my soul and are part of my story and soul's growth and evolution.

It was from seeing my father's determination and resilience when I was faced with my own health challenges and cervical cancer at 24 years old, that I was able to be an advocate for my health and well-being. This is a fundamental life skill that has stayed with me my entire life. A cause that is close to my heart is helping others become an advocate for their own health and to not accept what is handed to them as their fate – that they have more control over their health than they realise.

I have learned; that hindsight is a beautiful thing when you are able to use discernment with it, to always trust my intuition – about everything! I am always right about people and situations, sometimes it takes longer than expected for people to show their true colours, but it always comes out. To embrace my authenticity and sovereignty and that my life is mine alone to live and experience. People share the journey, but it is me who is always with me – no matter where in the world I am. To love all of me – the dark and the light. To never stop shining and dimming my light to make others feel better or because they are blinded and triggered by my light. To not take things personally, that everyone has their own silent struggles that you will never fully know about. The biggest life lesson – that love is the most important thing and that the meaning of life is that we are here to make an impact. The level of impact will look different for everyone and that is the magic of our life's purpose.

There is a real power in owning your story without being your story. When you can get to a point where you have healed enough from the situation to be able to talk about it in a way that it no longer owns you, takes over your mind, body or emotional state and can learn from the experience and meet it with forgiveness and compassion, your pain becomes your superpower. For me, this journey was one of the hardest roads I have ever taken – the inward journey. Navigating the deep dark depths of my soul, descending into the abyss of the unhealed and forgotten and shining a light on the shadow parts of myself. I can honestly say that this was the first time in my life I had given myself the time and space to truly sit within, to face myself and to make peace with what was and shower the pain, regret, shame, guilt and judgement with love compassion, empathy, kindness and self-love.

It was because of this moment in time of a major life event that I decided to make major life changes. I packed up my house and went on a deep soul journey, travelling through South America for 4.5 months. I journeyed on a deep inward soul discovery and reconnection in Costa Rica, met soul connections, sat with shamans, had private ceremonies in the mountains in Peru, connected back to nature in the Galapagos and the Amazon in Ecuador, experienced the diversity in Bolivia, chilled out in Colombia, stargazed in Chile and got soaked under the Iguassu falls in Argentina, danced every day and deeply connected to my feminine energy in Brazil, pushed myself in ways that I had never before and opened myself up to the unknown along the way. It was, without a doubt, the dream trip of a lifetime and I loved every minute of it! South America had been calling to me for many years and I always knew that when I visited, it would be for an extended period. What I didn't realise at the time was that this deep calling to visit this continent would be so integral in my healing journey.

I journeyed to and explored the deep dark depths of my soul and the hidden parts of myself and I sat fully with them. I unlocked the cage of purgatory I had kept myself locked away in for so long. Most importantly, I was able to allow myself the time and space for healing. I was finally able to breathe, move out of survival mode and feel like I was thriving! This journey didn't come from one significant action, it came from many – each layered and intricately linked – unravelling a layer deeper and deeper inward. The process started with learning about tantric embodiment when I hit burnout 10 years ago. I was so numbed out on all levels mentally, physically and spiritually that I needed to rebuild from the ground up and reconnect felt sensations. I then moved on to regaining physical health when I found colonics and juice cleanses, which were great for clearing excess toxins from the body and lifting my brain fog. The most significant deep healing came from plant medicine – Ayahuasca when I was at a Rythmia retreat in Costa Rica. Here is where I first discovered breathwork and the power of this brilliant modality. I truly felt like it lifted the lid on so much stored trauma I had locked away. Now breathwork is a part of my daily routine. I learnt and experienced first-hand that you can heal from trauma without reliving the trauma.

There had been many moments during my life when my soul was calling out to make changes, to heal, to deal, but I just wasn't listening. It was showing up through burnout, injuries or illness, lifestyle choices, relationship choices and the overall way I was living my life. I have spent a large part of my life living in survival mode. For so long, I didn't even know there was another way.

Knowing what I now know, I could have saved myself many years and so many painful experiences to be able to make changes in my life. Although I had tried through attending personal development seminars and events, I read books, meditated, sat in silence at Vipassana retreats, cleansed and fasted, used positive affirmations and whatever other resources I had. It still didn't seem to break through to that underlying layer – that layer in the subconscious that was playing out the same stories, beliefs and events over and over again.

Then, I discovered the work that I do now, and all of a sudden – the same positive actions and daily habits started to make shifts and changes. I could feel a different level of intent and energy behind everything I was doing. I started to experience rapid accelerations and changes – in all areas of my life! It was literally like I quantum leaped and merged into the new, future version of me that I had always wanted to be! Sometimes I still can't believe what my daily life looks like because it is so different from how it used to be.

I absolutely love to help my clients make change easy and bypass the years and hard work that it took me to be able to align with my life's purpose and live the life I always wanted to live. This work that I am doing is truly the work I am here to do and my legacy. I know that there is an easier way and I can help others biohack their way there too, making change easier and faster. Success leaves clues and when you follow the experts and implement the proven strategies, it is easier to emulate the results faster.

Change comes from change and it is through the incremental, daily shifts and habitual layer stacking that those big changes manifest. There is no magic quick fix, healing isn't a linear journey and the path looks different for everyone.

So much of my life had been lived people pleasing, with bendy to no boundaries and feeling like I had to be everything to everyone else and nothing for myself. I had lived my entire life feeling like I needed to fit a mould of what others expected from me, to be a perfect image of their ideals, like a chameleon changing from person to person and situation to situation. It was exhausting! I lost who I was, my soul essence was diluted and I was not living life for me.

By experiencing healing from trauma in a regulated way, I was easily able to move from survival mode into thriving and have experienced that it is possible to not only create the life of your dreams but live it every day. The fastest way out is through and for me, true inner freedom and real self-acceptance came from facing my inner demons. I was finally able to move forward in life, free from the past, free of the constraints I'd shackled myself in and free from inner and outer judgement and criticism. I was finally free to live in authenticity and sovereignty. My priorities in life changed and the way I need to live life has shifted. I now prioritise flow, ease and abundance over busyness, hustle and feeling like the more I work, the more I achieve. I have released the inner critic, embraced self-love and become clear on what is in alignment with my authenticity and sovereignty and now love to share this possibility with others.

Through the inner journey of shadow work, I came home. Rediscovering myself has been one of the most liberating and rewarding experiences of my life. Shadow work is integrating and facing the parts within that have been repressed, ignored or denied and is the traits, emotions or thoughts that create a level of discomfort, shame or guilt within. This is out of alignment with how we like to see ourselves or how we want others to perceive us. Everyone has a dark side, a repressed side and a part that holds the keys to true freedom – by facing and dealing with these parts.

By confronting and integrating our shadow side, you are shining the light on the darkness, truly embracing all of you and loving each aspect. This can be confronting and challenging work, but the rewards are life-lasting and endless.

If you need help diving into yourself on a deeper level and want to break free from your internal limitations, then please reach out. I offer a free discovery call where we can meet and discuss what is going on for you and the best treatment plan to help you move into the life you want to be living. You are worthy and deserving! For all readers of this book, you will receive a $250 voucher off your treatment plan *(T's & C's apply).*

BOOK FREE DISCOVERY CALL

Krista J. Sobieski

Founder of Thoughtful Seed Project

https://www.linkedin.com/in/krista-sobieski-12608326/
https://www.facebook.com/kjsobieski
https://thoughtfulseedproject.com/
https://unimaginablehope.org/

Krista Sobieski is the founder of the Thoughtful Seed Project of Central Wisconsin. A farmers wife and mother of four who has a strong background in early education, leadership development and community collaborations and loves to write and share her voice. She writes about topics including life, death, parenting, fundraising, motivation, and teamwork just to hame a few. Krista lives in the country, believes in the greater God, has worked in early childhood setting for 23 years. She is the founder of Unimaginable Hope, a non-profit charity with a mission to spread kindness and bring hope to those who need it. In a moment of darkness, Unimaginable Hope was created in memory of her parents, who she lost when they passed the same day, 3 hours apart.

Shielding Your Heart from Hurt When You Trust Unconditionally

By Krista J. Sobieski

Life is interesting. Born in the mid-70s, I do believe that I grew up in a time when life was simple, and sure seemed like it was a lot of fun. My childhood was fairly basic and my parents were what I would consider middle-class citizens, who worked hard, paid their bills, and only would ask for help if they really needed it; and they always paid their dues. They taught my sisters and me to put our needs first and wants second, trust in the good of people, and be responsible for ourselves.

I learned easily to trust people and believe in the good of people. I lived with neighbors who were like family and had family that was present, constant, and there for me.

My unforgettable personal story isn't a reflection of my life, but it's a reflection of my emotions, and how I learned to trust freely and believe in others. That seems like a positive thing and in many ways it is, yet, when you trust too freely, you can easily get hurt and allow others to walk all over you. When you go through trauma and other challenges, it can really alter your state of direction and clarity. You can quickly lose focus.

I have always felt as though I have been in check and balance yet my personal story altered my state of mind and has changed who I am. I allowed people to take advantage of my emotions, use my weaknesses, and hurt me. I froze when I had to stand up for myself and while I don't want to directly call out religion, I struggled to understand how I could allow those whom I thought were positive Christians to hurt me more.

Now, I am not naive to think people who identify as Christians are all perfect, yet I believe those who serve as role models and mentors will be supportive and understanding.

I was raised as a Christian and while religion wasn't a primary focus in our lives, it was present and as youth, we were raised to believe in God and the good of his teachings. I always found religion interesting and I would say my family was very laid back in attending church and continuing to push us as older teenagers. When I met my spouse, religion was very prevalent in his life and I was okay with that. I was eager to be more involved and make religion a larger focus in my life. While I would never push it on others or condemn them for not being religious, for me, I was grateful I had found a husband who found faith vital in his life. I felt like it gave me grounding for a way to live life, and eventually, raise my family. I felt connected.

To say I never questioned the bad things that happen in life, would not be the truth, yet I still remained faithful and believed in the good of people. I still trusted in people and the word of the Lord.

In 2016, my life started to become clouded. I had been happily married for almost 20 years and had four children, a career I liked, and felt like I was making a difference in the world. I was so excited about the future. Suddenly, I felt like things were starting to spiral out of my control. It seemed as though one bad thing happened and then another and another. The business I loved and was so proud of was now hurt by others, some of the people I trusted now seemed so distant, and my mother's breast cancer returned after the original diagnosis in 2011. It was a crazy time. I was being targeted to fix the issues in the business and my mom was terminally ill and dying. Then, when I thought it couldn't get worse, my mother passed and my father unexpectedly ended up having a heart attack three hours after my mom passed. It all seemed so unreal. That was my life and it seemed to be completely out of control. Well, the truth is, it felt like an out-of-body or out-of-soul experience.

I wrote about those experiences in my book titled *Giving into Hope*. It's an easy read and gives more insight into the specifics of going through those challenges, yet what I experienced following that traumatic time in my life is the disbelief, doubt, and lack of confidence that wears you down following traumatic stress. The hard parts of life were getting the best of me and I was allowing others to hurt me, yet what I didn't expect was the hurt of those who I thought would help comfort and console me, considering they were viewed as Christian people working in a religious environment. See, my Unforgettable Story is one that made me open my eyes to understand that sometimes the most unlikely people will hurt you. I don't know why I had on my blinders but I made a mistake by believing that people of faith won't hurt you. I know that was my heart wanting to believe that working in a religious-based setting would help take my hurt away. So much turmoil had happened in and around me, honestly, I thought that my faith would grow stronger working in and around those most deeply connected to their religion. I had worked in early education for nearly 23 years, dabbled in public speaking and hosting training, and loved writing so worked in the newspaper industry a bit, too. Yet, something inside me was calling me to look back to an environment that involved kids. It was a small private school and I jumped at the opportunity, though I knew it would be less money than I had ever made. The hours worked with our family schedules and it seemed like a place I could grow, not only in a career but in my faith. To me, it seemed like a win-win and the best part was that I could be part of making a difference in the lives of children and families, while supporting educators in the small role I played.

The position started out very well. Though everyone seemed fairly connected, and they were on point about helping children learn about their faith, it did not take long for me to start to feel and see the destruction of being part of a toxic environment. There were situations happening around me, again out of my control and when I started to feel confident in asking questions, I started to be shut out.

Nobody is protected from toxic behaviors or toxic people, yet it's so unexpected in people working in an environment that is supposedly there to teach and role model the Ten Commandments. Well, at least that was my thinking.

It started with the observation of school leaders being dishonest in serving students in need, watching money shift from one envelope to another without proper record keeping, and followed by really witnessing the divide of treatment of certain students and families being catered to and others not. Yet, despite the deception, with promises of tuition breaks, and glorified perks, the school had followers and those they needed to keep quiet and those they needed to keep happy, became very managed. I watched it on a daily basis and became concerned.

My promised wage increase was suddenly gone, my contract was no longer and there was no longer support on the difficult days. The communication between myself and my supervisor diminished and most days, it seemed like I was left out of the conversation. Despite several meetings throughout the year and questions asked, there were answers that were lies and if you didn't keep quiet and follow the leader, it did not become an easy place to work.

It almost became unbearable, yet in my mind, I did not want to believe that people of faith, especially people working and teaching children in a faith-based setting would be so hurtful. Not all people working there, remind you, were like this. This was primarily the administrative leaders.

As the school year started to come to a close, things started to heat up. I felt the tension, heard the broken promises over and over again and when I asked for meetings, despite getting them, in my heart I believed I was drawing too many red flags, and that was putting a snag in my supervisor's plans. She could no longer freely disrespect and use people and hurt them. Or could she?

I sensed our dysfunctional relationship getting more toxic, yet I felt a person of religious faith as she claimed, would be open to reason and allow a conversation to address my concerns and offer explanations for my questions.

Boy, was I wrong. When you blow the whistle, draw red flags, or voice your concerns, sometimes they will hurt you more, hurt you faster, and basically, you might question your own being and faith. Sometimes, it's hard not to see the good in people and when you want to believe that people are real, it's so hard to understand how they can hurt you.

My first mistake was going into an environment expecting it could help heal my own heart. That's on me for being loaded with traumatic pain to think working in a religious setting could bring comfort to my life. I do take responsibility for expecting that, though I won't take responsibility for how awful people can treat others and I still find it reclusive to think how awful people can treat others and how easily they can hurt them and toss them to the side like a dirty dish rag. Yet, we live in a kind of world, where it has become acceptable to allow greed and hurt to control our motives and we also allow others to easily hurt us.

As you can expect, the last blow-up happened with my supervisor and within a week of it, an email came with two paragraphs telling me I lost my job. I was so hurt. How could this person of deception maintain her role, though she didn't deserve to have it? So many trusting people, families, children, donors, and community members believe in the best like me, yet not fully on the inside, there was no way for them to see.

Eventually, after several attempts and connections to the church leader, he finally agreed to meet with me and I believed he would look at my notes, emails, and texts, the proof of the toxic behaviors, and just hear me out. I was wrong again. He told me I was being untruthful and everything I said was a discrepancy. It was unbelievable, unforgettable, but most of all, hurtful. How could so many turn their backs to allow this toxic behavior to continue? Several staff members were leaving as well and it just was an extension of my wanting to believe the best, yet allow myself to be hurt.

I quickly watched people turn away, people tell me that sometimes you have to just forget things and others tell me it was for the best to be away from that environment. Now I see how much better it is being away, though my heart still stings that my faith even had to be questioned because of the disregard and disrespect of another human. It hurts worse because this was to be someone I regarded as a person of good standing and good regard and who has others' well-being at interest.

I know that this is more about the people, than the religion and I have learned that despite wanting to believe the best in others, you sometimes have to walk away so that you don't end up hurt. Forgiveness and forgetting are two different concepts, despite both being actions. I suppose, just like me, my former supervisor had different experiences that led to her actions and perhaps, though I thought I wasn't strong, it was my inner strength and confidence that challenged her and drew into her weakness. Perhaps, it was still my heart working to seek the truth and find the good, that led me to see the worst. I still struggle to understand how others can continually hurt each other and if we really are seeking to be good Christians, then why can't we follow through to be?

I have been hurt, have experienced hurt, and know that I too have hurt others. Sharing this story will most likely upset some, yet in my faith journey, the only way to truly find the truth is to seek the truth and share it. For this story, I am sharing that was deeply hurt by people that I expected to help me grow stronger in my faith and when that didn't happen, it was unsettling and discouraging,

It did not make sense and again made me question my own self-worth and abilities. I allowed others' treatment to determine my emotions, to question myself, and to guide me down a path of self-destruction. We quickly let others hurt us and control us. Sometimes we let the world around us beat us down and seek answers that we already know.

I know that I expected more accountability from that supervisor and the church leader, and was seeking more than employment. I believed they could help me dig deeper and find greater religious balance and growth working alongside them. Was my expectation too great? Perhaps, yet now I find peace in believing that for those of us who believe we will face our redeemer, I believe they will too and their treatment of me will be questioned. Like most, I too have faults, make mistakes, and have had poor judgments, yet deliberately hurting others did cause me great hurt and these days so I try to look at it as a reminder of how not to act.

I have fully learned that we can not expect others to reward us with happiness and create our inner peace and strength. That is on us as individuals and only we can make ourselves happy. We all go through personal things that challenge and hurt us, yet holding on to the emotions of situations can hold us prisoners in our own minds and sabotage us from propelling us forward to live the life we deserve.

Life is funny that way. As that young girl born in the 70s and raised through the 80s, everything seemed so much easier. As an adult, it should not be harder to self-regulate and feel satisfied, though it's easier to accept that rarely individuals have a picture-perfect life. With time, allowing ourselves the grace to accept what we can't change, and understand that hurt and challenges are part of life, we can start to realize that we are more normal than not.

It took me longer than I expected to heal from the toxic supervisor. I am not sure if it was because of other past experiences or if it was because I could not overcome the fact she was so deceptive. In my mind, she seems to continue to have the opportunity to keep hurting.

Regardless, once I found myself in a better place and was able to focus less on the hurt and more on the acceptance of why I think it happened I was better able to gain focus on the positive aspects of my life and make changes that would never allow me to stop believing in myself when I am hurt.

I have learned to trust in my own instincts and seriously use my own senses to clue into what is happening around me and control what seems logical to control.

I cannot control how I am treated, though I can control my reaction. I have been emotionally drained in a controlled environment without a good vibe, yet I can attempt to remember that people are all different and come from different experiences. Despite being unable to know every person's background, it's not for me to judge, but rather become accepting to know that I am responsible for myself, not how others treat me. As a child, we are disciplined most often to protect us and to teach us limitations. When we are adults in positive relationships, and working in environments with positive managers and leaders, we are not treated unfairly or unjustly. It's important to have open, positive communication and when we feel a threat from toxic people, we shut down and shut up. I did this over and over again, partially because of the traumatic situations I suffered, and also had a feeling of being let down by others but again by the control and hopelessness I felt by those I expected to help me. I had a vision that Christian leaders should be supportive and engaging, yet the reality is, in fairness, we can't expect this from anyone. I have learned that to have the strength and courage to do what's right and speak up when there is a concern is very difficult, yet I wouldn't change doing it. Whistleblowing is necessary, if it's honest, and as much as I regret that others had a negative reflection of me and as much as it hurt to lose my career, I don't regret seeking change and trying to communicate my concerns.

I have also learned that despite feeling rejected, there is a place where everyone belongs. I felt very rejected by that specific school and church and had a hard time understanding that as they were to emulate Christian beliefs and actions in service of supporting people, yet they rejected me. It's a lonely feeling. Most people, even as adults, are more comfortable walking in a straight line, rather than wavering off.

As I age and life moves on, it humbles me. I no longer seek acceptance by following what everyone else is doing and while I don't want to be someone who rocks the boat, I will continue to be a person of integrity, who tries to do what's right and will still continue to love people. As a person with empathy, I will continue to respect that loving unconditionally will come at a cost; however, the disappointments will be far outweighed by the support and love you receive back.

Do not allow challenging situations and people to force you to become cold. I did. I was so angry and hurt and fell into a dark place out of frustration and felt like I was rejected so it caused me to shut down and stop trusting. It's okay to shield your heart and be guarded, yet it's sabotaging yourself of happiness when you let the disappointments and hurt overcome you. Here are some ways to overcome negativity:

Seek Support: Talking to a trusted friend or therapist can help process emotions. I waited six years to seek therapy or counseling for past trauma and it took toxic behaviors in the workplace to the point of feeling like something was wrong with me to get professional help.

Practice Self-Care: Engage in activities that bring comfort, like reading or spending time outdoors. For me, writing became a way to help bring peace and calm to my life. Find something that interests you away from what and who hurts you and get involved. Meet people who you connect with.

Focus on Healing: Allow yourself time to grieve and reflect, but also work towards acceptance and moving forward. Grief is not just about death. Grief can be about careers and relationships, too. Finding positive ways to overcome the hurt is necessary in the healing process.

Stay Positive: Surround yourself with positivity and affirmations to nurture a hopeful mindset. Try to find the bright side of things and continue to look for the good.

Embrace Growth: Use the experience as a chance to learn and grow stronger. It took me over a year to heal from my career loss and move on as I was in such disbelief that I could be hurt in that way, but I learned that no one is immune to being hurt. We will all be hurt at some point in our lives. As adults, we don't expect other adults to hurt us, but they do. Remember, others are mean because of who they are, not who you are. Hurt is caused by people who are internally suffering and unable to self-regulate. Do yourself a favor and find ways to help yourself grow and be an inspiration to others.

My unforgettable, personal story is mine and I hope that it inspires you to reflect on feelings, emotions, and how you allow others to affect you. Sharing is not about calling out others, it is more about how perceptions and expectations can put us in vulnerable places. It's everyday life, yet it can be really challenging and so often we go through situations in the workplace and in life that alter our state of mind. When you do, my hope is that my story will help you stay committed to believing in yourself and always try to stay focused in moving forward. Remember that rejection can be redirection and while in the moment it hurts, it also might be an open door to lead you down a new path that you were destined for.

Please consider reading my blog or my book, *Giving Into Hope*, available on Amazon or on my website, Thoughtful Seed Project. I am also the founder of a non-profit, Unimaginable Hope, a charity in memory of my parents, that has a mission to do good in this world. Other anthologies I am part of include Voices of 100: Women and Her Giving Journey.

Niurka Coteron

Unstoppable Being LLC & Insightful CFO, LLC
Business Growth and Wealth Strategist

https://www.facebook.com/niurka.coteron
https://www.instagram.com/niurkacoteron/
https://www.insightfulcfo.com/
https://www.unstoppablebeing.com/

Niurka Coteron is a distinguished business and growth strategist, transformation catalyst, and seasoned business mentor with over 35 years of notable career achievements. Excelling in executive leadership and global industry consulting across public, private, and non-profit sectors, she's left an enduring impact.

Author of "Begin From Within," available on Amazon, Niurka shines as a luminary in her field. Her international speaking engagements and collaboration with other women captivate audiences with profound insights. She is recognized with esteemed accolades and showcases extensive business knowledge and dedication to empowering women to become millionaires.

As Founder and CEO of Insightful CFO, LLC, Niurka expertly leads professional accounting and management consulting. Her firm helps business entrepreneurs make informed decisions and manage their financial operations effectively by identifying business gaps and optimizing operational excellence and profitability.

As the visionary behind Unstoppable Being, LLC, Niurka empowers women through coaching, workshops, and digital courses, fostering confidence, leadership, and intentional life design to make millions.

Her academic achievements include an Executive Master of Business Administration from Strayer University and Jack Welch Management Institute and two Bachelor of Science in Accounting and Finance from Rutgers University. She acquired a certificate in Women's Entrepreneurship from Cornell University. She holds various certifications in the financial field.

Breaking the Silence:
A Journey of Courage and Survival

By Niurka Coteron

At fourteen, my life was already a whirlwind of challenges and changes. I left Cuba as a political refugee with my father and three siblings, forced to leave my mother behind due to restrictions imposed by the Cuban government. We arrived in New Jersey, and the harsh reality of our situation set in: we were refugees, starting over with no mother, no money, no connections, and no clear path forward.

I was raised with high moral standards and constantly taught that I couldn't have sexual intercourse unless I were married, a belief deeply ingrained in my upbringing. A year after our escape, when most teenagers were navigating school and friendships, my life took another dramatic turn.

Witnessing my father's daily struggle under overwhelming responsibilities, I made a fateful choice. His weary eyes and slumped shoulders spoke volumes of the burdens he carried. In my naivety, I believed I had found a solution to ease his pain: marriage. I convinced myself that marrying my boyfriend of a few months, who was five years my senior, would lift a great weight from my father's shoulders. How wrong I was?

As I stood in that cold courthouse, clutching my father's calloused hands, I uttered promises I barely understood. I thought I was being noble, sacrificing my youth to alleviate my father's hardship. Instead, I was unwittingly stepping into a nightmare of my own making. What I envisioned as an escape from one problem became the beginning of a far darker journey that would test me in ways I could never have imagined.

My parents, bound by cultural norms and traditions, respected what they believed were my wishes. But what does a 15-year-old truly understand about marriage and lifelong commitment? Their own experiences led them to believe this union was the right path for me, a way to secure my future and perhaps ease our family's burdens.

In its questionable judgment, the New Jersey court system permitted us to proceed with this marriage. Their sole condition: I must not leave high school because I was 15. This agreement, meant to protect my education, would end up shackling me in ways I couldn't foresee. The ink on those court documents might as well have been chains, binding me to a life I was unprepared for.

My wedding was a small affair, attended by close family and friends. On the surface, everything seemed normal, but beneath the smiles and congratulations, I felt a growing sense of unease. I realized that I hardly knew the man I was marrying, and the reality of our age difference began to weigh heavily on my mind.

I felt an overwhelming dread as I dressed in my white gown on the wedding morning. As I stood in front of the mirror, adjusting my veil and trying to look happy, thoughts of not showing up flooded my mind. I considered running away, finding a way out of this situation before it was too late. But I wasn't afraid of disappointing my father; I was terrified of what my husband-to-be might do to me if I left him at the altar. With a heavy heart, I walked down the aisle, unaware of the darkness ahead.

A few days into the marriage, the cracks started to show. My husband, whom I'll call John for the sake of sharing my story, revealed a side of himself that I had never seen before. The charming facade he had presented during our courtship quickly faded, replaced by a controlling and abusive demeanor.

For nine long months, I lived in a constant state of terror. Every day, there was a struggle to anticipate John's mood and avoid triggering his wrath. The most minor mistakes, like not adding enough salt to the salad, could set him off. I felt like I was walking on eggshells, never knowing when the next outburst would occur. There were moments when he abused me simply because I got home past the arrival time he imposed. Additionally, I was taking birth control pills, and every time he found them in my drawer, he would discard them and throw them in the garbage, causing irregularities in my menstrual cycle and concerns about getting pregnant.

I was afraid to tell my father or anyone else about the abuse. I feared that if I spoke up, it would only make things worse. I believed that my father might confront John and escalate the violence. My internal nervous system felt broken, constantly on high alert. The fear and anxiety were overwhelming, and I began to feel trapped in a situation with no way out.

School, which had once been my sanctuary, became another source of stress. I struggled to keep up with my studies, but the constant fear and anxiety made it nearly impossible to focus. My grades began to slip, and I felt like I was losing control of my life. I couldn't confide in my friends or teachers, afraid they would judge me or, even worse, tell someone who might confront John.

The abuse took a toll on my mental and physical health. I often had trouble sleeping, and my grades continued to suffer. I lost weight and became withdrawn, no longer the vibrant, hopeful teenager I once was. A constant state of fear and anxiety replaced the joy and curiosity that had defined my personality.

One awful night, John came home drunk and more aggressive than usual. He accused me of things I hadn't done and started throwing furniture around the house. Another evening, I sat at the kitchen table, studying for an important exam. My textbooks spread out before me; I lost myself in the complexities of biology. John walked in and announced that he was hungry. Wanting to be a good wife, I immediately got up and started preparing dinner. I served him a plate of rice and steak but forgot to add the steak sauce on top.

What happened next still haunts me. John exploded in anger, yelling and throwing things around the room. He grabbed my books and began tearing them apart, the pages fluttering to the floor like fallen leaves. I stood there, paralyzed with fear, not knowing what to do or how to react. My heart raced, and my mind went blank. I had never encountered such rage before, shaking me to my core.

I locked myself in the bathroom, trembling and praying that he would calm down. In that moment of desperation, I realized I couldn't continue living like this. I had to find a way out but didn't know where to start.

Despite the fear and uncertainty, I eventually found the strength to seek help. The following day, I called a taxi and ended up at the police station in my town. There, I mustered the courage to confide, and with a shaky voice, I told them everything – the abuse, the fear, the helplessness.

The police officers listened without judgment and offered me desperately needed support. They helped me navigate the steps to leave my abusive husband, connecting me with resources and organizations that could assist me.

Further, they drove me to the county courthouse, where a judge listened to my case and placed an emergency restraining order mandating the police to remove him from our home. They also encouraged me to talk to my father, assuring me that he would want to know the truth and help me.

Telling my father was one of the hardest things I had ever done. With tears streaming down my face, I sat him down and told him everything.

To my relief, he was more understanding and supportive than I had ever imagined. He hugged me tightly and promised to help me get through this.

With my father's support, I filed for divorce and began the long journey of healing. It wasn't easy, but I slowly started to rebuild my life. I returned to school with a renewed determination to succeed, knowing that my past would not define my future.

The road to recovery was long and challenging. I had to move to another town where John couldn't find me. There were days when the memories of the abuse would overwhelm me, but I refused to let them control my life. I attended therapy sessions, where I learned coping mechanisms and strategies to deal with the trauma. I surrounded myself with supportive friends and family who encouraged me to keep moving forward.

As I regained my confidence and self-worth, I again began to excel in my studies. I graduated from high school and went on to pursue a college degree. My experiences taught me the importance of resilience and determination, and I was determined to build a better future.

Years later, I look back on my past with sadness and pride. My experiences were harrowing but also shaped me into who I am today. I am stronger, more resilient, and more compassionate because of what I endured. I have learned to value my worth and to never settle for anything less than I deserve.

My journey taught me the importance of speaking up and seeking help, no matter how impossible it may seem. It showed me the strength I had within myself to overcome adversity and reclaim my life.

Today, I cherish a happy marriage with a kind and loving partner. My spouse respects me deeply and actively supports my goals and aspirations. We've built a relationship founded on mutual understanding, trust, and genuine care for each other. This partnership starkly contrasts my past experiences, serving as a testament to the healing and growth I've achieved. Together, we forge a life filled with love, respect, and shared dreams, proving that past hardships don't define one's future. I hope that by sharing my story, I can help others find their path to healing and empowerment. I am one of the lucky ones.

I am one of the lucky ones because I did not suffer long-term consequences. Unfortunately, many of these children suffer devastating and lifelong consequences, including medical and mental health issues leading to depression, higher dropout rates from school, higher risk of pregnancy, poverty, and physical and emotional abuse from their husbands. We hope to end this harmful practice and protect vulnerable children by educating communities and advocating for policy changes.

Do you know that "worldwide, more than 650 million women alive today are married as children? Every year, at least 12 million girls are married before they reach the age of 18. This is 28 girls every minute. One in every five girls is married or in union before age 18. In the least developed countries, that number doubles: 40 percent of girls are married before age 18, and 12 percent of girls are married before age 15. The practice is particularly widespread in conflict-affected countries and humanitarian settings (source: **UNICEF**[1])."

Do you know that child marriage is still legal in 80% of the United States? Only 10 states have passed laws to ban child marriage and advocate lawmakers to end the practice. My state, New Jersey, only passed a ban on child marriage in 2018. "According to Unchained data, 10 states have a minimum marrying age of 17; 23 states have a minimum age of 16; two states have a minimum age of 15; and five states don't have a minimum age specified at all."[2]

Getting married before the age of 18 has limited legal rights, "even at the age of 16 or 17 are typically too young to leave home, file for divorce or even enter a domestic violence shelter even if a marriage turns abusive. Child marriage is more likely to happen to girls than boys."[3]

Also, it's not as if we wake up on our 18th birthday suddenly understanding who we are, what we stand for, or why we would choose to get married. I believe every woman should date various people while developing her identity and character. The self-development approach helps her understand who she is becoming and what qualities she would seek in a future husband. Once she gains a sense of wisdom and maturity, she will be better equipped to choose a life partner.

It's important to approach this topic carefully, as child marriage is a serious issue with long-lasting consequences. Here are some actions children can consider if they find themselves in a situation where marriage is being discussed or pressured:

1. Seek help from trusted adults: Teachers, school counselors, relatives, or community leaders who can advocate on their behalf.
2. Educate themselves: Learn about their rights, the legal marriage age in their area, and the potential consequences of early marriage.
3. Communicate openly: If possible, have honest conversations with parents or guardians about their feelings, fears, and future aspirations.
4. Contact child protection services: In many places, there are organizations dedicated to protecting children's rights and preventing child marriage.
5. Reach out to support hotlines: Many countries have helplines for children facing difficult situations.
6. Focus on education: Emphasize the importance of continuing their education and how marriage might interfere with this.

7. Seek legal advice: In some cases, consulting with a legal professional specializing in children's rights may be necessary.
8. Build a support network: Connect with peers or organizations that support children's rights and can offer emotional support.
9. Document the situation: If safe, record any pressure or plans related to marriage.
10. Have a safety plan: If there's a risk of being forced into marriage, consider having a plan to leave safely if necessary.

It's crucial to remember that child marriage is illegal in many countries and can have severe negative impacts on a child's health, education, and future opportunities. The primary focus should always be protecting the child's well-being and rights.

Here are some book recommendations that could be helpful for children facing the prospect of early marriage or for those who want to learn more about the issue:

1. "I Am Nujood, Age 10 and Divorced" by Nujood Ali and Delphine Minoui is a true story about a young Yemeni girl who successfully sought a divorce.
2. "It's Not Over: Leaving Behind Disappointment and Learning to Dream Again" by R. A. Dickey While not specifically about child marriage; this book discusses overcoming difficult circumstances.
3. "Half the Sky: Turning Oppression into Opportunity for Women Worldwide" by Nicholas D. Kristof and Sheryl WuDunn Includes discussions on various issues affecting women and girls, including child marriage.
4. "Sold" by Patricia McCormick is a novel about a young girl trafficked from Nepal to India, touching on issues of child exploitation.
5. "What Works to Prevent Child Marriage" by Margaret E. Greene: A more academic look at strategies to prevent child marriage.

6. "Just As I Am" by Cicely Tyson is an autobiography that includes Tyson's marriage experience at a young age.
7. "The Blue-Eyed Aborigine" by Rosemary Hayes is A historical novel that touches on cultural differences and early marriage themes.
8. "I Am Malala" by Malala Yousafzai While not directly about child marriage, it's an inspiring story about a young girl fighting for education and rights.

Remember, some of these books may contain mature themes. Young readers should discuss these books with a trusted adult who can provide context and support. Additionally, local libraries or women's rights organizations might have resources tailored to your region and situation.

Here are some online resources that can provide information, support, and guidance regarding child marriage and related issues:

1. Girls Not Brides (https://www.girlsnotbrides.org/) A global partnership committed to ending child marriage.
2. UNICEF Child Protection (https://www.unicef.org/protection/child-marriage) Information and resources on child marriage from a leading children's rights organization.
3. Too Young to Wed (https://tooyoungtowed.org/) is an organization that uses visual storytelling to raise awareness about child marriage.
4. Unchained At Last (https://www.unchainedatlast.org/) A US-based organization dedicated to ending forced and child marriage in America.
5. Childline (https://www.childline.org.uk/) A UK-based counseling service for children, which also has resources on child marriage.
6. Plan International (https://plan-international.org/protection/child-marriage/) An organization

working to advance children's rights and equality for girls.

7. World Vision (https://www.worldvision.org/child-protection-news-stories/child-marriage-facts) Provides facts and information about child marriage globally.

8. Save the Children (https://www.savethechildren.org/us/charity-stories/child-marriage-facts) Offers information and works to protect children's rights worldwide.

9. Human Rights Watch - Child Marriage (https://www.hrw.org/topic/womens-rights/child-marriage) Provides reports and advocacy on ending child marriage.

10. Youth Ki Awaaz (https://www.youthkiawaaz.com/) An Indian youth platform where young people often discuss social issues, including child marriage.

Remember to use these resources safely and privately if necessary. If you're in immediate danger, please contact local emergency services or a trusted adult for help. These websites can provide valuable information but are not substitutes for professional help in crisis situations.

My journey through child marriage and domestic abuse has fueled a lifelong commitment to advocacy. I now use my story as a powerful tool to raise awareness and empower other survivors to seek help. By sharing my experiences, I aim to break the silence surrounding these issues and inspire hope in those who may feel trapped or alone.

My advocacy work extends beyond simply sharing my story. I've taken on a leadership role as a board member for a nonprofit organization called Confronting Domestic Violence, Inc https://confrontingdomesticviolence.org. In this capacity, I'm actively involved in providing crucial support to victims of domestic abuse and their children. Our organization offers vital services such as relocation assistance, helping families find safety and stability away from their abusers. We also provide a range of other essential resources designed to support survivors, mitigate the impact of abuse, and work towards the ultimate goal of ending domestic violence.

I strive to create meaningful change through this combination of personal storytelling and direct action. My aim is not only to help individual survivors but also to challenge the societal norms and systems that allow child marriage and domestic abuse to persist. By confronting these issues head-on, I hope to contribute to a future where no one has to endure the hardships I faced.

Resources:

[1] https://data.unicef.org/topic/child-protection/child-marriage/

[2] https://19thnews.org/2023/07/explaining-child-marriage-laws-united-states/

[3] https://www.unchainedatlast.org/united-states-child-marriage-problem-study-findings-april-2021/

Connie Paglianiti

CEO of Connie Paglianiti

https://www.linkedin.com/in/conniemarieroberts/
https://www.facebook.com/ConniePaglianiti
https://www.instagram.com/conniempaglianiti/
https://conniepaglianiti.com/

Connie Paglianiti is a dynamic senior events and marketing professional based in Melbourne, Australia. With a rich career adorned with innovative event concepts and seamless logistics, Connie has excelled in creating memorable experiences that resonate globally. Her expertise spans across event production, audio-visual services, and exhibition management, with a notable presence in renowned venues like the Melbourne Convention and Exhibition Centre. An award-winning manager, she has successfully led teams in delivering high-value outcomes, ensuring every event exceeds client expectations.

Connie is also deeply committed to community service, speaking at various forums to advocate for resilience and recovery from gambling harm. As she prepares to launch her book and accompanying docuseries titled "Breaking Chains," Connie continues to inspire through her podcast, sharing stories of overcoming addictions and promoting supportive resources. Her approach, blending professionalism with passion, makes her a sought-after speaker and influencer in the event management and recovery communities.

From Shadows to Light: Empowering Second Chances and Breaking the Cycle of Re-Incarceration

By Connie Paglianiti

Introduction: Resilience as a Way of Life

As the sun rose over the sleepy Italian village of my childhood, the day's promise seemed as distant as the country I would soon call home. My story unfolds in a home shadowed by a diligent yet stern father, woven against a backdrop of stark poverty and the presence of violence. By the age of eleven, my life's tapestry was uprooted and restitched into the vibrant, daunting fabric of Australia. The transition was more than just a shift in geography—it was a voyage across cultural chasms and linguistic divides.

The early days were etched with the struggle of assimilation. English words felt like heavy stones in my mouth, and the nuances of conversation were as elusive as the whispering eucalyptus leaves that were so foreign to my senses. I sought refuge in the steady hum of my sewing machine, a comforting constant that rose above the turmoil encircling me. The rhythm of the needle and thread in my own hands became my silent language, a form of expression that needed no words to be understood.

Amidst the chaos of change, my hands moved with the certainty of legacy—stitching, mending, creating. What started as a means to draw thread through fabric soon weaved a path for self-sufficiency. I turned my skill into a secret enterprise, imparting my knowledge to other young girls in the neighborhood. The clink of coins in my pocket was a melody of independence, and with each lesson, I inched closer to the stage—a dreamland where I could sing my heart's unspoken words.

This clandestine pursuit was more than child's play; it was the dawn of entrepreneurial spirit and self-reliance. It was my silent declaration of defiance against the constraints of circumstance. Little did I know, this was just the first stitch in a lifelong pattern of resilience—a pattern that would come to define both the struggles and triumphs of my journey.

As life unfolded, each challenge was met with the same fortitude that had carried me across continents and through the invisible walls of difference. That young girl, who once silently sewed dreams into the seams of her reality, grew to understand that resilience was not just a response—it was a way of life.

Embracing New Horizons: A World of Possibilities

As I waved goodbye to the lingering echoes of adolescence, the vast Australian landscape became the canvas upon which my adult life would take shape. With each passing year, my accent softened, blending the lyrical intonations of my Italian heritage with the Aussie twang of my adopted homeland. I was caught somewhere between the warm, sun-baked cobblestones of Italy and the sprawling, golden beaches of Australia, and it was here that I began to map out the contours of my future.

Adulthood ushered in a mosaic of careers, each a colorful tile in the grand design of my life's work. I found myself exploring opportunities that ranged from the pragmatic to the creative. My days were as varied as the country's landscape, filled with unexpected roles and responsibilities that challenged my adaptability and rewarded my curiosity. It was in this eclectic professional journey that I discovered the thread that connected every endeavor: a deep-seated desire to contribute, to uplift, to mend not just garments but the fabric of society itself.

The pulse of charity work throbbed beneath the surface of my every pursuit. I recognized early on that my own challenges paled in comparison to the hardships faced by so many others, and this perspective became the wellspring of my philanthropic passion. Fundraising was not just a pastime; it was a calling. I championed causes with the same fervor I had once reserved for clandestine sewing lessons. The stakes were higher now, the audience larger, and the rewards infinitely more fulfilling. Every dollar raised was a testament to what could be achieved when compassion met action.

Travel, too, became an integral part of my narrative. With a solo traveler's tenacity, I traversed continents, each stamp in my passport a story, each journey an education. These adventures sculpted my independence and fortified my soul. The ancient ruins of far-off lands whispered lessons of impermanence, while bustling marketplaces taught the language of human connection beyond words. Unbeknownst to me, the resilience honed through these solitary sojourns was the training ground for the greatest test of fortitude I would ever face.

In the end, every job, every fundraiser, every solo trek across foreign lands was not just a chapter in my story but a preparation for the challenges that lay ahead. They were the proving grounds for my resilience, the arenas where my spirit was tested and strengthened, readying me for the unforeseen battles and the triumphs that would define my journey.

Finding Love and Building a Family

The journey of life often writes its own love stories, and mine was penned with patience. Amidst the tapestry of careers and ceaseless wanderlust, love found its way into my narrative in the most unexpected of chapters. I met my partner not in the flush of youth but in the full bloom of life, at the age of forty-two. It was a meeting of minds, of hearts weathered by individual histories, yet unyielding in the pursuit of happiness.

Our decision to marry was not bound by the traditional cadence of youth but was a choice made from the deep understanding that the right partner is timeless. Our wedding was an affirmation that love does not diminish with age; it deepens, it matures, it becomes a conscious choice of companionship and mutual respect.

Embracing motherhood at forty-five, I ventured into a world both wondrous and daunting. It was a late season to tread the paths of parenthood, each step a discovery, each moment a blend of awe and challenge. Motherhood after forty was not without its trials—there were whispers, there were doubts, but above all, there was an overwhelming sense of joy. Each sleepless night was a testament to life's miraculous cycles, each smile from my child was a reward for the wait.

These milestones, arriving later than society's script, granted me a unique vantage point. They illustrated that personal fulfillment need not adhere to a timetable. My life debunked the myth that there are definitive deadlines for love and family. Instead, it celebrated the idea that satisfaction and self-realization are journeys that do not follow a straight line but meander through experiences that are as richly diverse as they are deeply personal.

This era of my life reshaped my view on societal norms. It became clear that the conventions we often hold as absolute can stand to be challenged and reimagined. I learned that fulfillment comes from living authentically, from embracing life's opportunities whenever they may arise, and from the courage to build happiness on one's own terms.

The love that blossomed in the latter half of my life and the cherished role of motherhood brought into sharp focus the essence of what truly matters—connection, family, and the resilience to embrace life's gifts at every age.

The Unforeseen Turn: A Con, A Conviction, and A New Perspective

In the midst of life's upward trajectory, an unforeseen turn awaited me. A business venture embarked upon with trust and the promise of success, became the crucible of my greatest trial. I was betrayed by a partner, a con artist cloaked in the guise of professionalism and friendship. That betrayal spiraled into a nightmare that I could not have foreseen, leading to a conviction that threatened to dismantle everything I had built and stood for.

The emotional toll was immeasurable. Courtrooms became battlefields where I fought not only for my freedom but also for my identity and dignity. Each legal proceeding was a testament to my resolve, even as the weight of the situation threatened to crush my spirit. The gavel's fall marked the start of a journey I had never planned to take—a sojourn behind bars that would test and ultimately reveal the very core of who I am.

Life inside the jail bore little resemblance to the world I knew. It was a world ruled by a "country town mentality"—a closed-off ecosystem where outdated notions and prejudices loomed large, and officers held sway like small-town sheriffs presiding over their domain with unchecked power. Within these confines, I encountered bullying of a kind that was both petty and profound. Inmates, driven by their own fears and frustrations, lashed out at those they saw as vulnerable, and officers often instigated or turned a blind eye to such acts.

The challenges were relentless. But as had been my life's learned response, I met adversity with resilience. I sought solace in the very essence of what had always been my anchor—the inner strength that had carried me across continents and through life's many roles. I embraced strategies of coping that allowed me to maintain a sense of self. From forming alliances with the more empathetic inmates to engaging in introspective practices like writing and meditation, I fortified my inner defenses against the daily battles I faced.

I refused to let the environment systemize me, to reduce me to a mere number within its confines. Instead, I turned to education and advocacy within the jail's walls, sharing my knowledge and compassion with those around me, offering a beacon of hope and enlightenment where it was all too scarce.

This period of my life, so fraught with hardship, became a crucible that forged a new perspective—a vision clearer and sharper than any I had before. It was a vision of what truly matters: justice, truth, and the unwavering belief in redemption and second chances. It transformed my pain into purpose, and as I walked out of the institution that had held me, I stepped into a world where I was more determined than ever to make a difference.

Strength in the Struggle: Leading Change from Within

In the grip of incarceration, a reality that I had never imagined for myself unfolded. Yet, even as the heavy doors clanged shut, sealing me away from the world I knew, a fierce resolve took root within me. I was determined to resist being "systemized," to maintain my individuality against a system designed to standardize and suppress.

The struggle was not a solitary one. Surrounded by women, each with her own tale of despair, I saw the shadows that fell upon lives unlived, potentials unfulfilled. It was clear that while our freedom was restricted, our spirits need not be shackled. I made a silent vow: if the system would not change for us, we would spark change from within its very core.

However, this refuge was abruptly upended when COVID-19 swept across the globe. The pandemic, ruthless in its spread, did not spare the cold, stark world of incarceration. The virus brought everything to a standstill, including the educational pursuits that had become my lifeline. The structure and solace that learning provided were suddenly ripped away as the prison's scant resources were reallocated to stave off the health crisis.

Isolation took on a new, harsher meaning during the pandemic. The precious, albeit limited, visits from family—the gentle reminders of a life waiting outside—were replaced by infrequent and expensive phone calls or fleeting digital encounters on Zoom. The communal spirit that we had cultivated within the prison walls through shared learning and support was fragmented, leaving an aching void in its wake.

The world outside spoke of lockdowns and isolation, drawing parallels to our confinement. Yet, there was a stark difference between being locked down in the comfort of one's home and being imprisoned in a facility now even more isolated from society. While households turned inward, facing the pandemic with a semblance of normalcy, our reality was one of profound disconnection, with the programs that had provided a semblance of normalcy and hope for the future suspended indefinitely. As COVID-19 raged on, the silence of the halted educational programs in prison was deafening. The journey I had embarked upon—my personal investment in a future built on knowledge and self-improvement —was put on an indefinite pause. Yet, even in the face of this new obstacle, my resolve did not waver. The pandemic had taken much from us, but I refused to let it take my determination. With each day that passed, I vowed to hold tightly to the dreams I had been nurturing, ready to pursue them with even greater zeal once the world—and I—emerged from the shadow of the virus.

Despite the educational programs and communal activities grinding to a halt with the advent of COVID-19, my resolve for change within the walls of confinement remained unshaken. The once lively corridors became silent, but the drive to adapt and grow did not wane—it grew stronger. I was disconnected from my loved ones and from the support structures I had built, yet I found a connection in my experience of endurance through the pandemic.

It was in the quiet, in the stillness that wasn't chosen but imposed, that I found a deep well of strength. I saw that leading change from within wasn't dependent on the activities we could no longer participate in; it was about the resilience and unity I could foster despite them. Even as the world outside was changing in ways I could barely grasp from behind bars, I too was changing. I learnt to transform silence into reflection and separation into solidarity.

When I stepped back into the world, the landscape had shifted significantly due to the pandemic's impact. But the strength I brought with me was born from the challenges I had faced inside. It was a testament to my journey—a journey not of a standstill but of profound transformation. This passage through adversity was not the end but the beginning of a broader path I was now more prepared to tread—a path of advocacy, resilience, and ongoing reform in a post-pandemic era.

A New Chapter: Advocacy and Empowerment

My release from prison marked not merely a physical liberation, but the beginning of a profound personal transformation. Stepping out into the sunlight, the weight of my past experiences could have easily overshadowed my future. Instead, it fuelled a burning resolve to shine a light on the shadows that plague those who continue to serve their sentences, both inside and outside the prison walls.

I returned to a world vastly different from the one I had left behind, one where freedom was no longer a given but a gift. It was in this newfound liberty that I became acutely aware of the daunting challenges facing women upon their re-entry into society. Many of these women, lacking support and resources, found themselves caught in a relentless cycle of recidivism, not out of choice, but necessity. Their stories, woven with threads of regret, resilience, and an aching desire for redemption, inspired me to act.

Driven by the lessons of my journey and the hard-won strength from within prison walls, I embarked on a path of advocacy and empowerment. I envisioned a movement dedicated to breaking chains— literal and metaphorical—and to advocating for second chances. This vision crystallized into a concrete plan to assist former inmates in reintegrating into the workforce, not as marked individuals but as valuable, contributing members of society.

As part of this new chapter, I am currently pursuing a diploma in Event Management, which equips me with the skills to organize impactful community and fundraising events for this cause. Additionally, my engagement in a Key Speaker and podcast course is sharpening my ability to articulate the stories and truths that need to be heard, amplifying the voices that often go unnoticed.

My strategy involves not only advocating for systemic changes but also fostering direct partnerships with businesses willing to employ former inmates. I am committed to challenging the stigmas that overshadow the potential of these individuals. Through workshops, seminars, and public speaking engagements, I aim to transform public perceptions and corporate policies alike, advocating for a shift from exclusion to inclusion.

The core of my mission is empowerment through employment. By providing job training, resume-building workshops, and interview preparation courses, we prepare individuals not just to re-enter the workforce, but to thrive within it. The success of this initiative is measured not just in employment rates, but in the restored dignity and renewed hope it brings to those it serves.

This movement is more than a campaign; it is a commitment to alter the landscape of second chances. It is an ongoing effort to ensure that the doors opened upon release lead to paths of opportunity and not back to the gates of confinement.

As I continue to navigate this new path, my life is a testament to the power of resilience and the transformative impact of education and advocacy. Each day is a step forward in a journey of lifelong learning and leading change, driven by the belief that everyone deserves not just a second chance, but a real chance at a new beginning.

The Road Ahead: Challenges and Aspirations

As I stand at this juncture, looking back at the roads traversed and forward to the paths yet to be explored, I am filled with a sense of purpose and urgency. The journey has been long, marked by trials and triumphs that have shaped my understanding of resilience, transformation, and the profound impact of advocacy. The road ahead is laden with challenges, but it is also ripe with immense possibilities.

My aspirations are intertwined with the goals of the movement I am committed to leading. I envision a future where the stigma surrounding incarceration is dismantled, where society embraces those who have served their time with open arms and open minds. I dream of a world where second chances are genuine—where they lead to opportunities for growth, fulfillment, and contribution to society.

This vision is ambitious, but the steps to achieve it are clear. We must advocate for systemic changes that go beyond superficial adjustments to address the root causes of recidivism and social exclusion. Education must play a central role, not just within the confines of correctional facilities but as a cornerstone of reintegration into society. Employment, too, must be more than just a means to an end; it should be a gateway to a new life, offering dignity and a sense of purpose to those eager to make the most of their second chances.

To the readers, communities, and leaders who share this vision, I extend a heartfelt call to action. Support the initiatives that provide education and job training for former inmates. Advocate for policies that facilitate reintegration and encourage societal acceptance. Together, we can forge a path towards a more inclusive and rehabilitative future, one where every individual has the opportunity to contribute meaningfully to our community and reclaim their place in society with pride and support.

Ellen Forbus

Strategically You
Life Coach

http://facebook.com/StrategicallyYou
https://www.instagram.com/StrategicallyYou
https://www.strategicallyyou.biz/

Ellen Arsulic Forbus is a native of Northeast Ohio, has two sons, a fabulous daughter-in-law, and a precious grandbaby. Her career in the financial services sector has spanned over 40 years.

Ellen is looking to transition to retirement and desires to continue helping people via her life coaching practice. She became a certified life coach in 2014, after a few layoffs and consolidations in the banking industry. These skills also aided in better relating to her customers and their money mindset.

Ellen's coaching focuses on navigating life by knowing yourself better. She has lived through many pivotal moments and looks for the lesson in each, whether good or bad. Sometimes, you can't see the good in things when pain still lingers. Acknowledging the pain and moving forward are part of life and promote healing.

"Living the life of your dreams isn't just about dreaming,
it's also about living." —Mike Dooley

Getting Stuck in Life

By Ellen Forbus

Even though it was only around 5 o'clock in the afternoon in late May, the shadows cast from the tall trees in this remote section of the Loire Valley were starting to grow long and I could feel my anxiety start to creep in as I was searching for my hotel.

According to my directions, I was very close. Too bad the rental car's GPS wasn't working when I picked it up. Up until now, it wasn't an issue. However, here in the less populated part of the country my cell service wasn't working, so I couldn't use my cell phone's GPS.

I knew I was on the right road. I just had to find the correct turnoff. What's this? A big sign with banners and flags – oh, it's just a golf course. Not quite what I'm looking for.

My travel agent had booked me at a real chateau – Chateau Sept Tours – translated as Seven Tower Castle. I was so excited to be staying in a real castle. Truly a dream come true and I was so excited to stay there, if only I could find it.

There were lots of little side streets, actually more like country lanes really. I slowed and looked at each sign, trying to recognize some words that may be the place I was looking for. Slowing up wasn't an issue. This country road, while nicely paved, was not exactly a heavy-traffic area.

Finally, growing tired of looking and sure that I must have missed it, I turned down one of those country lanes. There was one house, on the corner as I turned. A cute little house with pretty flowers and a lady planting more flowers in pots in the backyard.

As I continued a short way down the lane, I realized this was turning more into a tractor path to access the farm fields. I decided I needed to turn around. Instead of just backing straight up, I thought I had enough room to pull up a bit, then back up a few times and I would be turned around.

It had been raining a light mist off and on the last few days. The mist had no effect on my touring for the week. In fact, the rough sea, overcast skies, and rain when I visited the D-Day beaches in Normandy gave a more realistic view of what the morning was like when those brave soldiers landed almost seventy years to the day I was there. The moody clouds gave the cemeteries an extra solemn vibe, especially the German cemetery, where the headstones were stark reminders of casualties on both sides of the war. Most of these German soldiers were in their teens.

This morning, I left my 16th-century Hotel Montgomery by Mont St. Michel, an abbey on the Atlantic coast that was built over 1,000 years ago, and drove through the rural Loire Valley on the way to this Chateau/hotel. I made a few stops along the way, like the medieval village of Fougeres where there was a quaint little town adjacent to a castle that was in partial ruin. The main part of the castle was intact and illustrated life in the 1400s complete with wall tapestries depicting hunting scenes that did double duty. They were decorative, but their primary role was to help keep the rooms warm and insulated, along with handmade tiles decorating the floors and around the fireplaces.

From there, I stopped for lunch at another village and then started to make my way to this evening's accommodations. The mist had been following me all the way from the Normandy coastline.

While I was trying to jockey my car around in this little lane, I noticed how soft the edges of the road were from all the rain. I pulled forward and put the car in reverse again knowing that this last little bit would get me completely turned around. As I stepped on the gas to back up, the front tires started whirring and mud started flying.

What? No! Don't tell me I'm stuck! I threw the car back in first gear (got to love European cars – they are all manual transmission unless you pay extra for automatic. I grew up driving stick shift and had really enjoyed handling a manual shift vehicle again) and the tires now spun mindlessly in the other direction. A few more thrusts from reverse to first and then I put the car in neutral and turned it off.

Sitting for a minute, my mind raced. Then, my forehead hit the steering wheel and the tears flowed.

What to hell did you think you were doing, trying to drive in France? Why are you here alone, anyway? You're such an idiot. I could see the sneer on my ex-husband's face as my mind continued to race about why I was here. The divorce was fresh – two days before I left for France. I thought the timing was perfect. Run away from the past, get my head on straight, and find myself. Find myself I did – IN A DITCH! And on and on. My brain took control and kept berating me for the mess I was in.

Finally, after what seemed like an eternity of despair that blanketed my brain, I lifted my head off the steering wheel and wiped my eyes. My practical Capricorn nature came back and took control. Nothing was going to get me out of this ditch if I kept sitting there scolding myself. I got out of the car and surveyed my situation. There was no way I would be able to get this car out by myself. Typically, you need someone pushing to rock the car while another is in the driver's seat going from reverse to first gear and back and forth. I have lived through many a Midwest winter – it's something you learn to do at a very young age!

Turning to face the main road, I walked to the little house on the corner of the lane that I passed when I turned in. The woman was still in her yard, planting flowers.

"Excusez-moi, pouvez-vous m'aider?" I said in my best French.

Startled, she looked up. "Bonjour!" She replied. "Qu'est-ce que vous avez?" Hello, what's up she said, looking me up and down. She obviously didn't notice me turning up her lane and probably was wondering where I came from.

"Parlez-vous anglais?" I said, asking her if she spoke English. "Pas tres bien." Not very well, she admitted.

Between French and English, I tried to explain my situation, that I was looking for my hotel and that my car was stuck. Suddenly she said "¿Habla español?"

"Sí, hablo un poco." I replied. Just another sign of the weird twists this day was taking. We added a third language, and it was enough to help us figure out what was going on.

In her lilting French accent, she told me her name was Marie Angel, and I smiled and told her my mom's name was Marie and that she was my angel for being home and helping me. She let me use her bathroom and gave me a glass of water while she called the hotel and a tow truck. The hotel, it turns out, was that highly decorated golf course with all the flags and banners – the hotel name was a little sign barely visible underneath! If only my travel agent had told me it was also a golf course! (Note: In reviewing this place for this chapter, it is now called Chateau Golf Sept Tours! If only that were the title then.)

The tow truck driver said he would probably be about two hours. The clerk at the hotel was named Tunni. Funny name I thought, until I realized that his name was Tony but the French pronunciation sounded like Tunni. Tony was a serious, studious-looking young man who was so concerned that he drove down to see if I was truly ok. He told me he would get my luggage out of my car and transfer it to his car to have it in my room whenever I got there. Tony was in his early 20s, I found out later, and was a student at the university. I thought he was very kind and conscientious for him to drive here to ensure that I was ok and to get my luggage. I wasn't sure that many 20-year-olds back home would have that kind of concern or care.

He was getting ready to walk back to my car when the tow truck driver showed up. It had only been 25 minutes! I was so happy that I didn't have to wait longer. We were all standing by Marie Angel's house, and they were all talking in French. A surreal fog was creeping over me, the conversation seemed miles away and it felt like all the words were coming through on a foreign radio station that I couldn't understand. While I caught some of the conversation, I was not a part of it until the tow truck driver said, "C'est loin?"

My brain snapped back to the present situation.

"Ce n'est pas loin!" I blurted out. All the chatter stopped. Everyone turned and looked at me and then cast furtive glances at each other. It felt like perhaps they had been talking about the dumb *Americaine* who got her car stuck. We started to walk back to the car, which was just out of view down the lane.

The tow truck driver took a quick look, clicked his tongue, and said it would cost me 225 euros to "clarer les pins" or get the tires unstuck. I nodded my head and said "Oui, j'ai l'argent." He turned and walked away, soon reappearing in his truck.

Tony, Marie Angel, and I stood to the side and watched as he hooked up my car, then got back in his truck and pulled it out. The job was done quickly, and aside from a lot of mud on the front end, no damage was done to the car.

The four of us again stood there, and again they all started conversing in French. I could feel myself slipping away again, their voices fading. This time, it was because I looked down at the ground, and right in front of my foot was a four-leaf clover!

Bending down to pick it up, I twirled it in my fingers, gazing intently at its significance. Once again, all conversation stopped as they watched the crazy *Americaine*. Then, clutching my prize good-luck symbol, I shook Marie Angel's hand and thanked her profusely in all three languages, expressing my appreciation for her help. I tried to pay her and she shook her head back and forth. "Non, non, I am just glad I was home. I am not usually home at this time of day."

The tow truck driver collected his euros and with a quick *merci* he turned, got in his truck, and drove off. Tony waited for me and told me to follow him. We made a left onto the main street, retracing my drive back to the golf course with the small sign announcing the hotel, Chateau Sept Tours.

As we drove back to the chateau, I realized I was shaking. What an escapade I just had. I followed Tony into the chateau and he stopped at the front desk to get my key. He then walked me and my luggage up the steps. I was staying in a turret room! My room was in one of the round towers – how magnificent! I thanked Tony, then turned around and decided to take a nap before dinner. The afternoon had been quite an adventure!

I woke to the sound of a cuckoo clock. But then I must be dreaming – it went way past 12 and it was still light out so it couldn't be twelve midnight and I know I didn't sleep until 12 noon!

It took a few minutes for the grogginess to wear off and I realized that here, deep in the forests of the Loire Valley, there must be a real live cuckoo bird! His haunting cuckoo echoed across the forest. How cool is that? I've always been fascinated by cuckoo clocks and now I'm listening to the real live bird.

I stuck my head out the window to better hear the bird. A light mist was falling again. I inhaled deeply the aroma and freshness of the damp forest; such a clean and wonderful scent of nature.

Looking at the time on my phone, I realized that it was time for me to get ready for my dinner reservation downstairs.

Feeling refreshed after getting washed up, applying fresh makeup, and changing clothes, I could feel my spirits rise. Had today really happened? One look at my car in the parking lot and I was assured it was no dream – the mud was caked on the undercarriage, tires, and front of the car.

Of course, dinner was by myself, like it was every night while I was traveling. That is the downside of traveling alone. Many times I can strike up a conversation with someone to help pass the time and learn about the other person, but tonight with this being a golf resort there were only a few couples having dinner and they put me at a table a little bit away from everyone else. Maybe they felt sorry for me? Maybe Tony told them about the crazy *Americaine* picking four-leaf clovers? Who knows!

The events of the day were roiling around in my mind. I had carefully planned every step of this trip. I had a map of every place I was going in case my phone did not have a signal. I spent the last six months planning this trip to a T. How did I not know the chateau housed a golf course? The planning was a diversion to my pending divorce. I immersed myself in this trip, deciding to drive myself instead of taking a tour. Tour buses are like Noah's Ark – everyone gets on in pairs, and I was no longer a pair. I imagined myself sitting with my head against the window, having pity party after pity party. Driving would take my mind off of things. What a great idea! Now I wasn't so sure. I still had many cities and miles to go. What other trouble could I get into?

There would be no other trouble. I decided this event had a lesson for me and I was going to figure it out. Besides, I grew up in the country driving all kinds of tractors and other vehicles, as long as I didn't make another poor decision, I would be fine.

The four-leaf clover was a highlight. And I know it was part of my lesson to learn. It was a sign from my Aunt Helen who had just passed away in the prior November. She was telling me that I was truly lucky and to keep looking for the good in life, just like she had always looked for four-leaf clovers. And the magic happens when you unexpectedly find a four-leaf clover, like I had today. What magic lies in store for me? The magic of going home alive and not dying in a ditch in some strange country? Stop! There is a lesson here, I kept telling myself.

Halfway through my meal, the sun came out for one final goodnight before setting behind the tall forest trees. With the light drizzle still coming down, the sun's rays splayed across the water droplets and formed a rainbow. Another good luck sign! My fork clattered on my plate. Everyone stared at me. Yes, the crazy *Americaine* is trying not to laugh in the middle of the dining room!

A four-leaf clover AND a rainbow? I slowly swirled my glass of wine. I pondered the treasures and the events of the day. Then I realized that these treasures were signs that there is always a positive side to life and mine, after surviving being stuck in a ditch on a tiny lane in remote France and having three kind people help me get back on my way WAS the answer. If I keep my wits about me, I can do anything even when things seem impossible. Even when life literally has me stuck – in a ditch – I can and will survive.

Being stuck in a ditch was symbolic of being stuck in life. If you let your Mean Girl brain, as Melissa Ambrosini calls it in her book, *Mastering Your Mean Girl Mind*, you are defeated.

This revelation was not really about the ditch, although that reality stared at me every time I looked at my mud-covered rental car. It was about surviving life, a divorce, and the death of three loved ones in the last ten months. It was about being resourceful and not letting things get me down. So I spent 225 euros on a tow truck – who needed those beautiful French-made leather shoes that I saw in a store window? This was life! How many other women would be adventurous enough to drive themselves around France for three weeks? Or should that be stupid enough? No, it is adventurous. Stupid is when you don't take calculated chances. Stupid is trying to back your car up the way I did! But the choice to drive was not stupid.

My total miles traveled during those three weeks was approximately 1,800 miles. I started in Paris, went to the Normandy coast, and then meandered through various regions until I ended on the Mediterranean coast in Nice. Immersing myself in the French culture, I managed to slow down my normal dizzying pace of life. I tasted great wine, cheese, and other regional specialties and talked to many kind people. I truly experienced the magnificence and beauty of France. Every chance I could, I would have someone take a picture of me with my good camera. You can tell that this event was a pivotal moment in the trip. The pictures taken prior to this event showed me with a tight-lipped smile trying to just have a historical accounting that I was in a certain place.

After this event, my pictures had a smiling woman with a new story to tell, one of not just a pivotal moment in a carefully curated trip, but a pivotal moment in life where she realized that life was to be lived, and yes there would be mistakes made along the way.

You don't have to spend three weeks driving in France to learn how to get unstuck in life. Granted, it is not as easy as having someone use their truck to get you unstuck, but it is absolutely more rewarding. With coaching, self-work, and self-care, you can train yourself to look for the positive, to quiet the monkey brain that is only too quick to point out all your faults, and live the life of your dreams.

Michelle Eshelman

Founder of Michelle's Virtual Adventure
Virtual Assistant

http://www.linkedin.com/in/michellelangdon23
https://www.facebook.com/michelle.langdon.56
https://www.instagram.com/virtual_assistant_adventures

Hi I'm Michelle Eshelman, an entrepreneur, from Indiana. I am a proud mother of an amazing 3 year old son. Life has been one difficult hurdle after another, however I want to share how these hurdles have made me who I am today and how I continued to push through...exhausted, defeated, hopeless, and sometimes with no resources. I see myself as an ordinary woman who refused to accept my fate that my life would be filled with abuse, drugs, uneducated, and unhappy. I am an ordinary woman who is willing to die for extraordinary principles, who continues to pound the stone without seeing results immediately. I am an ordinary woman who wants to show others no matter where you are or where you come from this does not have to be your future your fate. From one ordinary person to another, YOU got this!

Eighteen – More to Life

By Michelle Eshelman

Eighteen, legally an adult, car packed with what little I had, off to college. So many thoughts, so many emotions. Am I making the right choice, how am I going to survive, am I going to fail, wow I am actually doing this, and the thoughts go on.

Not many know my background, my upbringing, all the struggles I have faced in life, and how hard I have always had to fight. Nothing in my life has ever come easy to me. I feel I wasn't supposed to graduate high school, let alone be off to college, but here I was, a High School graduate off to take on this big world!

When I speak about how I was not even supposed to graduate high school, I say this because my mother, my biological father, my younger sister, and now my younger brother never graduated high school. I had to work and study really hard for good/average grades, I dealt with bullying and struggled with confidence. I did not have a relationship with my biological father, there was constantly arguing going on in the house along with other challenging situations, and wondering if all my current struggles would be how life was going to be moving forward.

This is going to be the hardest to get out, something that very few people know about me but I feel I need to share because I pray that I can truly help someone with some of my story as hard as it is to share. When I also speak about how I was not even supposed to graduate high school, I mean I truly did not think I would be alive.

When I was about 15/16 years old, I truly believed that life was not worth living and that if this was truly what life was going to be like I did not want to suffer through any more of it. I wanted out. Whatever would happen after I was gone had to be better than what I was living through and what I had to look forward to in life.

One night I decided to just start taking as many ibuprofen as I could and just drift away. I started to drift in and out. The next thing I remember is being at the hospital. I was still drifting in and out. I remember having to drink a charcoal-type drink instead of pumping my stomach after that I was out until the next day. I remember only having one person come visit me besides my family being there. I remember returning to school and for me, my world had stopped and I did not know what to think of still being alive. Yet, watching the world go on like nothing happened was very eye-opening.

I am not sure what I expected to happen. That suddenly all the bullies in school would realize what they were doing was wrong, that boys would stop cheating, that my home life would suddenly change… It was this day that I realized that I had more control than I thought, that the world did not owe me anything and if I wanted my life to be better, I had to do something about it.

I truly believe that mindset matters! I consistently heard and thought "you will never be able to do that," "we do not have the money for that," "it's not possible," and "you won't be able to make it." As much as I felt stuck, as much as I thought this is how life is and what I was dealt just had to deal with it. I have been blessed to have a few people in my life who saw how hard-working, coachable, full of life, inquisitive, and wanting more from life helped me along.

My mindset began to shift from just dealing with what life threw at me to there is more to life. I opened my eyes and really paid attention to others around me. These women were showing me what is possible, encouraging me to look at options, keep my head in the game, and at least graduate high school.

Junior year of high school, I had to switch schools. In some ways, this was a blessing, in other ways, this just sucked! So close to graduating and the people I had known for years and thought I would be graduating with were now in my rearview mirror. I was starting over, credits and class levels were different, and new people, most of whom, grew up together and have been friends with for years. Here I am, the "new" kid scared to death of everything and everyone. So many things changing in life with my parent's divorce, who I would be living with, where I would be living, changing schools, different outlooks on life, on top of the typical teenage life dramas of my hair sucks, boys suck, two-faced fake friends, trying to figure out what you truly enjoy, and while others had been preparing for college and what life would look like after high school I was just trying to survive.

A bit of quick backstory is needed to move forward. I do not have a relationship with my biological father as he was using drugs and an abusive person. My mother made the choice to leave when I was very young. We were blessed to have met a wonderful man who married my mom and later adopted my sisters and me. So, when I refer to my father, I speak of my adoptive father as he has been the only father figure since I was 5 years old; however, they did decide to divorce while I was in high school.

When I changed schools there was one thing I was looking forward to. I had a female cousin who was close to my age and we had always gotten along at family gatherings and often wanted more time together. Well, this was my only hope of surviving the last bit of my high school years, or so I thought.

The excitement was very real at the beginning, woo-hoo, isn't this what we always wanted? Soon, I was being introduced to all her friends and getting the "lay of the land" of high school clicks. I didn't feel so alone at this point and was hopeful that I could make it through the last few years of high school not lonely and an outsider.

Well, quickly this changed when I was being referred to as the "hot new girl" and a boy asked for my number who happened to be the boyfriend of my cousin's best friend. I had no idea who he was and that they were dating. I did not follow through but even then not doing anything wrong but just purely existing, I was immediately hated and bullied by my own cousin for nothing I did but how others saw me. This was her school and she was sick of hearing about "the new hot girl."

I was now not only alone again but also being bullied. My anxiety was so bad that between passing periods I would run and have to slow down my breathing in the bathroom and collect myself to go to class. I kept to myself and then people began saying I was a "stuck-up" person and was too good to talk to anyone.

The rest of high school was not all bad. I worked to keep decent grades and I was able to do a work-study where I only went to school half a day and worked the rest of the day. This allowed me to start saving up to buy my first car and to start saving for my future whatever that looked like. So let's just say, when it was graduation day, I was happy in many ways to walk across that stage and walk away from high school. This was what I was waiting for, this moment right here. I was legally an adult and was free from school if I chose not to further my education. This is where my life is going to truly change, I am truly and legally allowed to make my own decisions.

We do not choose where we are born, we cannot always control how we are living under the age of 18, but we can control how we react. We can choose to reach out to others for help and advice, and not be so stuck in our lives to realize all life's opportunities that truly are out there no matter the hand you were dealt.

So there I was, almost nineteen, legally an adult, car packed with what little I had, off to college. So many thoughts, so many emotions. Am I making the right choice, how am I going to survive, am I going to fail, wow I am actually doing this, and the thoughts go on.

I remember looking in my rearview mirror crying and feeling like I was doing something wrong, what if my family needed me, I see what life has to offer, maybe I should stay and try to help more, maybe I am not good enough for what I am chasing, I certainly won't fit in at college, am I going to be the only one working and going to school, what will people think of me I drive an older car and have older clothes, and will this be a repeat of high school?

I soon dried my tears and switched my mindset. I had a lot to think about in the 2.5-hour drive south to my new hometown. Wow, this is such a freeing yet scary feeling. I needed to follow my dreams, chase goals, and know failure is a part of life and means I am at least trying.

Months back, college did not even seem like an option. I had decided I wanted to go tour colleges, look at costs and options of how I would afford to pay for schooling. After a few tours, looking at the dollar signs, and not 100% sure on what I really wanted to study. I quickly began to give up hope. People like me do not get the chance to go to college. I was ridiculous for having this dream and thought that I could do this.

People have been prepping for years and here I am just jumping in and going to try to make this happen on a whim. This feeling sucked and I was beginning to understand why some have the mindset of not going after things because they did not want to get their hopes up. Also, the reason behind telling someone there is no way to even try was to possibly try to protect them.

I was not giving up hope, I started with higher hopes and dreams but realized there were still other options. I was determined not to give up until I found a way to go to college. This is where I realized I could start at a college such as Ivy Tech, especially, not being 100% sure what I wanted to major in as well as how was I going to pay for college.

I researched and applied for FASFA government grants. I was awarded grants due to my parent's low income and I began applying for any scholarships I qualified for. To this day I look back and giggle at the fact I was so determined I found a scholarship that asked me to write about if I found an alien would I be its friend.

Through research, hard work, and determination I applied to Ivy Tech, received an acceptance letter, prepared finances, and signed up for basic courses such as English and math. I was on my own, scared, but determination kept me going to ask questions and figure it out.

I was blessed that my grandmother agreed to let me come live with her as I was getting prepared for my first semester at Ivy Tech College with hopes of transferring to Ball State College. I needed to find a job immediately. Luckily, there were many restaurants and serving opportunities around so I quickly found a job.

Next on the list was to determine what I really wanted to study and "do" with my life. I started thinking of careers most people respected instead of listening to my heart about what I enjoyed. I started chasing after goals that weren't really mine to chase, just for the approval and validation of others and the world.

I started as an accounting major and quickly found numbers were not for me. I switched and flipped flop on majors. I then landed on child education to become a kindergarten teacher. Teachers were respectable, others valued teachers, and I, honestly, did love children.

Ball State had a great teaching program so switching over majors, and knowing I wanted to eventually transfer over, was fitting. I completed a few semesters at Ivy Tech to then apply at Ball State. I knew I wouldn't get into Ball State unless starting at a smaller college due to money as well as my academics.

AHHHHHHHH, the letter finally came. I had been accepted to Ball State after making the dean's list multiple semesters over at Ivy Tech! Hard work and determination were paying off. I had been working almost full time as well as going to school full time. There were times I felt I was missing out on typical college learning experiences such as living in the dorms and going out but I was so driven and focused on what I needed to do to be able to continue my education as well as pay bills.

I eventually was able to rent a place with a few other college ladies, helping build my confidence and making me feel I was accomplishing more but getting out on my own more. I did hit some rough times as I had a roommate that was stealing money and I ended up losing financial aid. Looking back, man, that was a tough time as well, but I overcame it. I was on the phone for hours and sending emails until I was able to appeal and receive financial aid again.

I continued on and I remember getting into the student teaching process in my degree. I absolutely loved it and received so many compliments stating I was a natural and this was where I was meant to be. I had reached out to current teachers as I was now working in childcare and asked what they had thought of actually being in the classroom. Some stated they loved it but what I heard over and over was it was also tough because of state standards and pressure on hitting certain goals, not having funding to do more creative activities, or having time for them.

I know with everything in life there is always going to be some type of challenge but I was nervous about getting in the classroom and it being so different from what I was currently doing and not being able to bring joy and happiness to my class. I had also had some comments from people very close to me who I really wanted them to approve of what I was doing and showing them there was more to life. When these hurtful comments were made I realized maybe I needed to pursue a harder, more respectable career.

So even though I was very close to graduating with a major in childhood education I went to my advisor and figured out options. I had enough credits to graduate with a major in general studies with concentration areas in early childhood education and health science. So I said, let's get me graduated and I want to now start down a path to an associates in radiography.

Surely an x-ray tech will show everyone I am hardworking, smart, and make good money. The program is hard to get into. Let's do this. I graduated college in May 2015. I got to walk across another stage; another milestone. I applied for the radiography program for the fall with around 50 applicants and only 4 spots!

Another letter... Ahhhhh, did I get in, am I finally going to get my chance to prove to everyone I can do this and I can "make it" in life? I GOT IN!!! This felt amazing but reality also set in how am I going to pay for this, I cannot work or work much being a full-time student and full-time clinic hands-on in the hospital, but I have to work because I have bills to pay.

Again, I got busy because where there is a will, there is a way. I am not a quitter, I have always found a way so I am not about to quit now. Well, I was blessed to have figured out a way to get a scholarship to cover the cost of the program but now how was I going to make money? I realized I made good money serving at restaurants but I could not work that many hours. So I connected with a friend who told me about a bar job where I can make really good money while not working many hours. I applied and went for it no matter how uncomfortable it was. I had to do this to make it work with the program.

Here I am, chugging along at classes and clinics. I thought it would feel different but I did not feel that fire in my heart as I did with teaching. I was interested in what I was learning and doing but I felt I was there for the wrong reasons. Did I really want this or was I doing this to appease others?

I found the answer to this about a year in. Two students were kicked out due to grades and one dropped out. I was the only student left but at this point, I was not in a good spot. I was guessing everything I had done so far and I hated the bar scene. I hit a point where I was again thinking this is my life, my choice, is this my chance to do what makes me happy in life so why am I here?

Shortly after realizing what I was doing wasn't going to change the thoughts of others about me. No matter what I did in life, some people were never going to approve of what I was doing because I was fighting against staying stuck in how I grew up and wanting more in life. Fine, I'll take the title of "stuck-up" and continue fighting to figure out a happier and healthier lifestyle.

I dropped out of school, quit the bar job, and started therapy. I felt so lost and stuck in a deep dark hole. I had kept myself so busy and had not processed so many life events that I decided I needed to start there. I need a safe space to just unpack all my life events and figure out where to go from here. I couldn't have felt more like a failure at this point in life but I knew I would figure it out somehow, someway.

I slowly started making progress in therapy, I knew I needed to work again and decided to start down the path in the banking world. I was starting to slowly climb out of that dark hole of depression and confusion. I was really truly thinking of what I wanted from life and what would make me happy. Reminding myself it doesn't matter what anyone else thinks, at the end of the day I am living this life so what do I want?

I continued on with banking but was not passionate about this career choice. I also was dreaming of the mountains and moving out of state. I had always moved around but always in Indiana. I knew there was so much more than life in Indiana. At this time I had met someone special in my life who shared the same interest in the outdoor lifestyle and moving out of state to the mountains. He had an opportunity for a job out in Idaho, we flew out together, and we both loved it! He asked what I thought and I said let's do this!

We ventured out to the absolutely beautiful state of Idaho to just absorb everything we could from life! What a ride that was! We got engaged, married, and had an amazing boy, who is now 3 years old! Our little Idaho spud!

There were many ups and downs out there but it was life-changing in so many ways. Maybe a future book to dive deeper but I encourage everyone to get out and explore as much as possible. It was a different way of living out there which I truly enjoyed.

It was a scary big life-changing adventure. I did not have a job moving out there but I knew I would figure it out. I did not want this to stop me from having this life experience. I sent in job application after job application until finally, I was back in scrubs! I had landed a job as a medical assistant, and funny enough, helping in the surgery center drawing meds and running the x-ray during surgeries. I really enjoyed this opportunity and this time it was for me not for a title or anyone else. I was truly making choices based on what I wanted in life.

Fast forward to my 30th birthday! Yes, the actual day of my 30th birthday! I was rushing around getting ready for work realizing, hmmm, I should have started my period by now. Well, I had to use the restroom before rushing off to work, and I happened to have a test.

I was in total shock, I was pregnant! Very unexpected but what an exciting start to my big 30th birthday! I knew life was about to change in so many ways. One big thing was that as much as I loved what I was doing, I never had the flexibility, as my husband and I missed out on life due to having to work but had to work to live. At this time, there were more and more opportunities to work from home or more flexible positions out there. Finding out I was pregnant lit a fire in me to figure out how I was going to work from home and raise this child.

I already did not want to miss out on life opportunities now more than ever. I wanted to take full advantage of life with this new life but knew again I had to still have an income. While working full time I began researching how to work from home. I came across the opportunity of Virtual Assisting. I dove head-first in and got to work. No matter what, I will be working from home by the time I have this baby!

You guessed it! My determination, willpower, and my continuation to take advantage and live life to the fullest. I made it happen! I was exhausted from being pregnant, working a full-time office job, and working part-time or more to get a business up and running.

Taking that leap of faith and realizing I had to step out of the office job to fully make this business work. Two months before the arrival of our son, I did it! I am now a business owner! I am now working from home! I finally have the flexibility and freedom I had been searching for.

I felt on top of the world and then life hit! Life hit so hard, all at once, and so unexpectedly. I had thought I had gone through some tough times before… Life said watch this!

Postpartum, my adopted father, the only father I had ever known, a man who changed my life, passed away unexpectedly, my marriage was falling apart, I had no support, I couldn't take care of myself, I had this precious little child that needed me, and I just crumbled!

I made sure my sweet baby had everything he needed and was taken care of. I don't know how I did it but my body kept going even when I felt like I didn't want to take another breath. He needed me and I would never abandon him!

I worked, I took care of him, and I took care of the household. One day, I came across the opportunity for a wild women's retreat. I knew I had to do this. I needed to do something for myself. I needed to process the death of my father, try to get some sleep, clear my head, and figure my life out once again.

On this trip to Alaska, I met some of the most amazing women who helped me grieve the loss of my father, realize I was not in a healthy safe marriage, and made me realize I needed to take my life back yet again.

Returning from this trip I was able to come back out of my fog, love my little guy, and jump into my business again. I had also dove more into my marriage in hopes that there was something there to save. More than anything I wanted to keep our family together but I knew I needed to start setting some boundaries and I prayed we could get through this. I learned no matter how much I wanted our marriage to work I could not do it alone. It was not just about my husband and me anymore. There is now a precious boy involved that deserves the world.

In last-ditch efforts to save our marriage, I suggested we move back home to Indiana. Maybe being around family and more friends would help. Unfortunately, things continued to get worse and I knew there was no saving this marriage.

Divorced and starting over. Life is full of the unexpected but it can be beautiful if you let it and find those beautiful things. I will never stop trying to better my life as well as my son's life. I will never stop trying to help others see the beauty of life through the hard times. I will continue onward and upward.

I have been so blessed to have started my business years ago to allow me to get through all the struggles in life. I truly feel this is where I belong and I am doing what I was meant to do. No, I am not a doctor, lawyer, or x-ray tech, but I am a mother, I am a business owner, and I help others. I am proud of myself through all the failures and achievements and I will continue to stand proud through more failures because I know it will be another lesson on what to do differently and better.

I have continued to face many challenges in life, as many do, but I am a fighter, I am a survivor, I am determined, I am kind-hearted, and I want to help others. You may see me fail and fall but you will never see me stay down!

I truly hope to you reading this, I have touched you in some way, I have given hope when you are feeling hopeless, I have helped speak to you to let you know this is your life you only get one, take control of it, and don't be too afraid to try and be afraid of never achieving anything at all because you are too afraid of what others will think of you.

I hope you will think "what if?" for yourself by watching me fail and get back up over and over again. I hope you start to realize your happy ending is staying soft despite how the world has tried to defeat you, embracing change, moving and growing forward. I hope you know that we are not responsible for other people's poor behavior, that is on them. What is on you is how you choose to respond, set your boundaries and know your worth!

Lastly, my words to you.

Doesn't matter, do it anyway.
Doesn't matter, find a way.
Doesn't matter, just start.
Doesn't matter, follow your heart.
Doesn't matter, just don't give up!

Susan Heartlight

Heartlight360.com
Spiritual Director

https://www.linkedin.com/in/susan-heartlight-a287a730/
https://www.facebook.com/groups/1332654857099489/user/100000660748017
https://www.instagram.com/nolaheartlight
https://heartlight360.com/

Susan Heartlight, born in New Orleans, January 23, 1954; to her native New York parents, James White a Chiropractor and Doris White a Cosmetics Buyer for D.H. Holmes. Susan is the oldest daughter with two sisters; three younger brothers and two older brothers. Susan dreamed of having a dozen children with a great husband/partner and chose poorly attracting men with as much baggage as hers. With little support from her family and no self-worth or self-esteem; she was knocked around in the river of life.

By the age of 27, Susan had given birth to three daughters and a son and found herself to be a single mother doing her best to manage it all. Two dysfunctional marriages that ended in divorce and with little education, Susan returned to school at the advice of a social worker; to become a better person and mother. Life provided challenges and rewards!

My Unforgettable:
Personal Stories That Will Inspire You

By Susan Heartlight

When I was 10 years old, we lived in New Orleans, two blocks away from a small park with giant oak trees. We didn't have cell phones or social media. We barely had television and radio. Children played outside and used their own imagination. The oak trees had large branches that reached down, low to the ground, as if they had arms reaching down encouraging us to climb on for an adventure.

My parents were at work and my brother Ronny was a young man working and partying so he was barely home at all. There was no one home to watch over my two sisters and me. The trees made me feel safe. I climbed up those branches to the center and felt this mighty oak hold me. High above in the center of its branches, I could see people coming and going. Children laughing and playing, riding bicycles, and other people walking their dogs. I was invisible.

Then one day we moved and my father no longer lived with us.

Self-Worth

As an innocent child, I was not concerned with self-worth. I lived in the moment as long as I was outside and not inside my home. My world inside with my family was gray, not bright or dark. We were raised by parents who moved all the time and they did not understand the concept of parenting.

I barely even knew I existed until we began to attend the New Orleans Bible Church. The minister spoke about Jesus. He said, "Jesus healed people, loved everyone, and believed we were good." I didn't really hear about sin, hell, or damnation. The minister said, "If you want to be close to Jesus you can be baptized and he will be inside of you and with you all the time." I thought that was terrific! I wanted to be just like Jesus and love everyone. I asked if I could be baptized and the minister said I needed my parents' permission. My parents said yes, so, I was baptized on October 24, 1964, at the age of ten.

I loved musical theater and was in the play, Oliver Twist, at the age of eleven. One evening I was waiting on the streetcar, which ended at the intersection of Carrollton and Claiborne Ave. where we lived. My childhood home is no longer there; nonetheless, the streetcars are still there today. The streetcars are connected by a metal pole to wires above it and run on a steel railway. They have beautiful wooden benches and the back of the bench moves so that it always faces in the direction you are headed. I was alone on the streetcar that evening on my way to a rehearsal. I heard a voice as clear as someone sitting next to me. "Everything that happens to you will be to help someone." I was perplexed and looked around; however, I did not see anyone. The words are engraved in my mind. From that moment on there was a fight for my soul. Because I had chosen the Light, the dark side wanted me even more.

Unknown to the adults, there was a pedophile working on the corner, preying on innocent children who were not being protected. Children without a father, or a mother who worked all the time, or an older teenage brother who worked to help out his mother and was rarely ever home. This pedophile was the newspaperman. Mr. Mike was what we called him. The intersection on the corner had a soda counter inside of a drugstore and all the kids would get off the bus and buy a soda and French fries. I never had any money because we were poor. If I helped Mr. Mike sell newspapers, he would give me money. Somedays, a quarter to buy a soda, and some days a dollar twenty-five to buy a soda and French fries. He was always there during the day, he always smiled and was happy to see me. Then one day, he said I could make more money if I helped him clean his house. Then Mr. Mike would ask me to do things that felt weird and I did not understand at all. Things to my body. Things with his body. I didn't want to go clean his house anymore.

My father had an office in Jefferson where he also lived. I loved playing the violin and my teacher felt I was good enough and gave me private lessons in his home. My teacher lived very close to where my father's office was. After my private violin lessons, I would go down the street and see my father. I loved my father and felt special because I got to see him. My father betrayed my trust and did things to my body. I was his little girl. Why did he do those things? I loved my daddy. Why did he want to confuse me? I stopped going to my violin lessons and never played again.

The police came to our house and asked questions about Mr. Mike. I was terrified. I thought I had done something wrong and they were going to take me away from my family. They asked me if Mr. Mike had bothered me. I was so afraid I said, "No." My mother never spoke about the incidents and moved us far away to Algiers, Louisiana. Mom was gone longer from home because we lived further away from her jobs. Mom would take a bus on the corner of our street to the Algiers ferry, over to New Orleans, and then walk several blocks to D. H. Holmes, the department store where she loved to work. She worked extra side jobs babysitting for the hotel guests and for an ice cream store on the weekends. My older brother, eventually, moved away closer to his job in Avondale. My sisters and I had no one except our elderly grandmother who lived a few blocks away in an apartment above a store. My sisters and I were 13, 12, and 10.

Within that first year, a college boy named Jimmy befriended me and we would sit on the sidewalk cut-through between the houses and talk about everything. He was handsome and five years older than me. He told me he liked me. I was barely 14 now and a skinny little twig of a girl. One day Jimmy said, "Do you want to see my house?" He lived in a nice upper-middle-class area and I was excited to go. He brought me over and asked me if I wanted a drink. It looked like Coca-Cola. The last thing I remembered was him handing that drink to me. I blacked out. I didn't know it at the time but he had put something in my drink.

People were banging loudly on the door and the walls!!! Jimmy shook me and told me to crawl from the bedroom to the bathroom and put my clothes on. I didn't remember taking my clothes off. In the bathroom, I felt funny and I was giggling as I got dressed. I felt kind of numb. I came out and Jimmy was sitting on the couch holding a shotgun. I sat next to him. He was shaking. He said he had called his friend Randy to come by to see who was outside. Randy told Jimmy that it was my mother and sister banging on the door. Jimmy walked me to the door. I didn't want to go. Jimmy told me I had to go. I got into the backseat of the car with my mother and sister and we drove home in silence. My mother never spoke to me about it. She blamed me and shamed me. A neighbor girl down the street from our house liked Jimmy and told them I was there with him. I don't know what else she told my mother and sister. They never spoke to me about it.

I was completing the eighth grade ready for summertime. Bob was in one of my classes at school. He liked me. Bob and I went to hang out at the library with the kids from school. Bob's older brother Mike was sitting in a car outside. Bob and I walked over to say hi and his brother looked at me. I thought he was cute and he was older. Two years older. Bob had a very nice sister, Alice. I would ask Alice if I could come over and visit so that I could see Mike. Then Mike would take me for rides in his car. Mike and I would go park under a tree in Behrman Park to kiss. Mike liked to drink Old Grand Dad, straight bourbon whiskey. One time I asked Mike if I could taste it. It was strong to me and I didn't like it. Mike did more than kiss me that night.

Mike and I were driving around and I felt sick. Mike got me some water and I threw up. Mike got me some soda and I threw it up. Mike said, "I think you have morning sickness." I said, "What is morning sickness?" I was clueless. My mother never talked with me about sexuality. The class in school was not realistic and did not make any sense to me. It was in black and white with a circle for girls and a line for boys. The line went in the circle. There was no anatomy. What does this mean?

I was pregnant at 15 years old! I didn't show and had no idea what to expect. One day during the summer we went to the beach and I wore my bikini and my mother noticed my bump. She was devastated and within days brought me to a building where they give up children for adoption. I told her I did not want to give up my baby. My mother then sent me to live with my oldest brother in St. Louis. That did not last long. Gordon and I were not close. I felt like he was a bully.

It was 1969. I came back to New Orleans (Algiers) and went to live where all the kids used to hang out, at the Stones House. The mother was always home and she didn't care if you smoked or drank or whatever. My room was very tiny but I didn't care. I remember playing football with all my friends and feeling fine, with a big belly. I hung out at another neighbor's home and one night I had a sharp pain. I was going into labor! It was my mother's birthday. They called her and she came to pick me up. We drove in silence as I squirmed in pain riding across the Mississippi River bridge to the hospital. The Sara Mayo Hospital at the end of Jackson Ave. near the river is no longer there. My mother walked inside with me and then the hospital staff took me in. The nurse said to my mother, "Say goodbye to your baby," as my mother was not allowed to be inside with me.

I was in pain and terrified! The nurse took me into an empty room. She told me to get up onto a metal table. She shaved my pubic hair, gave me an enema, and said, "I'll be back in a few minutes." She came back and brought me to the bathroom. I was in a panic thinking that I would have my baby in the toilet. Then she brought me into a birthing room and I do not remember anything after they gave me a "Twilight drip," and I counted backwards from ten saying, "Ten, nine…"

My mother was told it took four people to hold me down when I was giving birth. When I woke up, I hurt down there. The nurse told me I tore and they had to put in stitches. She placed a heat lamp under my covers. A while later they brought my baby girl in to meet me. I freaked out! I was traumatized! I was still under the effects of the sedation. My sister gave me a present with purple paisley designs on it and I freaked out again. It took a day or two to get the sedation out of my body.

I had no idea how to be a mother. I never played with dolls. I did not feel nurtured by my own mother. My little sister loved my baby and wanted to play with her.

Becoming

My story goes on many paths of naivety and learning about life through hard knocks and tsunamis. My request is for mothers, grandmothers, and aunties to speak to the young women and girls today, informing them of sexuality. Our young women need to understand their bodies and how pregnancy occurs. Informed young women need to be educated with real anatomy, so they will not become victims. Young women, you are worth understanding relationships and being treasured by others. Women have incredible bodies that carry the future generations to come. Know what your choices are and how to take care of yourself. Seek out information from older women and counselors. You are worth it! Enjoy your young tender years and may you have parents that look out for you and speak with you about life. Life is wonderful.

I know my youth was turbulent; nonetheless, I turned out okay because something inside of me kept me aligned with the good in the world. I had many years of close calls with people who use people and could have easily been in a nightmare lost to drugs and severe abuse. I will share some of those stories another time. I thank God for protecting me. Good conquers evil. The Light conquers the darkness. Always choose Life because there are many twists and turns and just around the corner there is a good person who will encourage you to become the greatness that is already within you!

Who Am I?

I did not know who I would become. There is greatness in each one of us just like the acorn has a mighty oak tree within – we each have a purpose and dreams inside of us to give to the world and ourselves.

I became many things before the one thing that gives me joy. I became a waitress, hostess, barmaid, soldier, dental assistant, massage therapist, Reiki Master, deli clerk, bank clerk, bookstore clerk, volunteer for the battered women's shelter, intern for rape crisis, suicide prevention, the YMCA's Project FOCYS, and a psychiatric hospital. After thirteen years of education and passing the written and oral exams I became a Licensed Marriage and Family Therapist. I worked in private practice and for the Center for Independence of the Disabled, the County of Siskiyou Behavioral Health, and finally with the Los Angeles Superior Court.

The voice that spoke to me as a child is still with me today. "Everything that happens to you will be to help someone." Everything I do is to help someone. Never give up on your dreams. The giant oak trees took many years to reach its branches down and lift me up to the center of its safety. Focus on what you want. Write it down. Find pictures of it and cut them out. Make a map of your life with your picture in the center. Look at it every day. Whatever you hold in your mind will manifest into your life!

My books are available on Amazon and I hope you reach out to me because I would love to write a personal message inside your book and autograph your copy. https://heartlight360.com

Sonya McDonald

Founder and CEO of Sonya McDonald LLC
Board Certified Transformational Life Coach, Registered Nurse,
Author, and Speaker

https://www.linkedin.com/in/sonya-mcdonald-rn-bsn-bcc-7786521b9/
https://www.facebook.com/sonya.mcdonald.96/
https://www.instagram.com/sonyamcdonald_/
https://www.sonyamcdonald.com/

Sonya McDonald is a much sought-after expert as a Board-Certified Transformational Life Coach, Author, Speaker, and Registered Nurse with 30 years of experience. She received her Board Certification as a Life Coach from Robbins Madanes Training Institute, the official coach training school of Tony Robbins. She dedicates her life to empowering women to conquer fear, rise above overwhelm, confidently embracing a life of authenticity and fulfillment. Living with Rheumatoid Arthritis and Fibromyalgia for over 16 years, and anxiety since childhood, Sonya proves that chronic and invisible illness does not define you. When she's not spending time with her two beautiful daughters and husband, or walking her dog, Sonya loves ocean sunsets, swimming, and immersing herself in nature. Let her guide you, igniting your inner light and helping you shine brightly, no matter the challenges you face. To learn more about how Sonya can help you, visit her website at www.sonyamcdonald.com.

The Awakening Within

By Sonya McDonald

The world around me blurred as the searing pain in my chest tightened its grip, each breath a desperate, agonizing struggle. Feverish and drenched in sweat, I stumbled into the hospital, gasping for air that seemed just out of reach. Nurses rushed to my side, their faces masks of urgent concern, as they wheeled me into the depths of the emergency room. Machines beeped frantically, echoing the chaos in my mind as I realized the gravity of my situation. In that moment, the harsh reality hit me: I might not make it out of here alive.

Once in the emergency room, the medical staff assessed my condition with swift precision. They placed me in a double isolation room, the result of a new protocol due to the outbreak of a mysterious virus that was spreading globally: COVID-19. The room was bare and sterile, its walls a blinding white that seemed to absorb all sense of comfort and warmth. The air was thick with the scent of disinfectant, a constant reminder of the invisible threat lurking around every corner. The double isolation measures meant that I was completely cut off from the outside world. No visitors were allowed; not even my closest family members could be by my side. The door to my room remained closed, a barrier that seemed to solidify my growing sense of isolation. The only human contact I had was with the medical staff, who entered my room in full protective gear, their faces hidden behind masks, shields, and gowns. The anonymity of their appearance made the experience even more surreal and unsettling.

Days stretched into an eternity as I lay in that isolation room, battling the unrelenting fever and struggling to breathe. The ceiling became my canvas, a blank expanse where my mind projected fears and memories. The constant beeping of the heart monitor and the hiss of the breathing treatments were my only companions, their sounds both a comfort and a torment. Each cough racked my body with pain, my lungs burning with each labored breath.

The absence of visitors made the experience even more distressing. I longed for the familiar faces of my loved ones, for the comfort of their touch and the sound of their voices. The phone calls and video chats, while a lifeline, could not bridge the gap of physical presence. The isolation weighed heavily on my spirit, amplifying my fears and uncertainties about my outcome. Each passing day felt like a battle fought in solitude, my resilience tested in ways I had never imagined, like a candle's flame enduring the passage of time, its unwavering glow a testament to inner strength.

In the depths of my despair, I turned to prayer. Alone in the sterile isolation room, I prayed to God for strength and guidance. The act of praying provided a sense of peace, a feeling that I was not entirely alone. I poured out my fears, my hopes, and my determination to survive. In those moments of prayer, I felt a flicker of hope ignite within me, a reminder that there was still something to fight for. Then, a miracle happened. The hospital made an exception, allowing my daughter to visit me. It was on her birthday. She entered the room, gowned and masked, her eyes filled with concern and love. They were pools of compassion reflecting the depths of her love. With each glance her eyes whispered words of encouragement, painting pictures of healing and strength. Seeing her was like the sun breaking through the clouds, its rays casting warmth and hope into every corner of my soul. The physical presence of seeing her was an indescribable gift. Her visit became a turning point for me. It reignited my will to fight, to get better, to leave that hospital room and return to my life at home with my family who I loved and missed so very deeply.

The resolve to strengthen my immune system became a personal mission. Having lived with Rheumatoid Arthritis and Fibromyalgia for over sixteen years and anxiety since childhood, I knew that I needed to handle my health and mindset differently. This experience was a harsh reminder that I could no longer be passive in my approach to wellness. I needed to make significant changes to support and enhance my weakened immune system and my overall emotional and physical health and well-being. The week following my daughter's visit was marked by a renewed sense of purpose. I began to visualize my recovery, focusing on what I would do once I was out of the hospital. I knew that managing Rheumatoid Arthritis, Fibromyalgia, and anxiety required a holistic approach. It wasn't just about treating the symptoms; it was about nurturing my entire being. As an RN for over twenty-eight years, I had the knowledge and experience to understand the complexities of chronic illness. But this time, I needed to apply that knowledge to myself in a way I had never done before. I started by educating myself on holistic health practices, seeking ways to enhance my immune system and overall well-being.

Diet was the first area I tackled. I researched anti-inflammatory foods and began to plan meals that would nourish and heal my body. Fresh, whole foods replaced processed and sugary options. I discovered the benefits of ingredients like turmeric, ginger, and leafy greens, incorporating them into my daily diet. The changes were not easy, but the positive effects on my health were evident almost immediately. The biggest realization that I stumbled across was at my first Tony Robbins Unleash the Power Within virtual event that I attended in July 2020. Anthony Williams spoke on celery juice and the holistic healing properties and effects it has on our bodies. I never knew at that time how powerful this one vegetable could be on my entire body. I decided at that event that I would commit to drinking this celery juice every single day and just give it a try. It has truly been life-changing for my health. Not only has it decreased my pain and inflammation, but it also helped with reducing migraines and controlling my blood pressure. I was able to reduce some of the medications I had been taking for years and learn to live well with my disease of Rheumatoid Arthritis and Fibromyalgia. I am not in complete remission, but it has significantly improved.

Exercise became a vital part of my routine. I found activities that were gentle on my joints but effective in building strength and stamina. Yoga, with its emphasis on flexibility and mindfulness, became a favorite. Swimming and walking also became integral parts of my regimen. Each movement was a step towards reclaiming my physical health.

Mental wellness was equally important in my recovery. Have you ever been so overwhelmed in life and stuck, and it felt like a dark cloud was hanging over your head and you were sinking in quicksand and could not catch your breath? Well, I sure have with my health issues, all the uncertainty that happens in life, and my racing anxious thoughts. I learned to quiet my mind, focusing on the present moment rather than being consumed by worries about the future. Mindfulness, prayer, and meditation became daily practices, helping me manage my anxiety and maintain a positive outlook. I learned to do deep breathing techniques and listen to calm music to also help calm my nervous system. These practices provided a sense of peace and clarity, grounding me in the reality of my progress rather than the uncertainty of my fears. The mind is so very powerful and having a positive mindset was a game changer in reducing my anxiety and all my health and life challenges.

Gratitude became such a powerful tool. Each day, I practiced gratitude, focusing on the things I was thankful for rather than dwelling on my limitations. This shift in perspective helped me see the progress I was making, no matter how small, and it fueled my determination to keep moving forward. I vividly remember my first walk outside after returning home from the hospital. As I watched a baby bunny hopping playfully through the grass, a smile spread across my face, as if the sight of its innocent joy mirrored my own newfound sense of freedom and hope. The sun beamed brightly overhead, birds sang sweetly, and I breathed in the fresh air, surrounded by nature's awe-inspiring beauty. This sense of gratitude I felt for the simple, yet profound, experiences in nature became a crucial turning point in my journey towards self-discovery and inner freedom. Another powerful tool I discovered in my life was journaling. I began journaling which created a sense of calmness and peace in my life which I had never experienced like this before. Journaling provided a sanctuary, a quiet retreat where I could pour out my thoughts and feelings, much like a river finding its way to the sea. It was a process of unburdening my mind, releasing the pent-up tensions and worries that had accumulated. Through this practice, I began to uncover patterns and insights, much like a scientist conducting an experiment. Writing became a mirror reflecting my true self, helping me see connections and understand my motivations more clearly. Journaling provided a rhythm and structure to my days. It was a grounding ritual, a moment of stillness where I could pause, reflect, and gain perspective. Each word written was a step towards greater self-discovery and freedom and allowed me to release my anxious thoughts from my mind, like a diver emerging from the depths of the ocean with treasures that sparkle in the sunlight.

Support from family and friends, even though limited to virtual interactions, was invaluable. Their messages of love and encouragement were lifelines that lifted my spirits and reinforced my resolve. Knowing that I was not alone in my journey provided a sense of community and strength. As I continued to heal, I realized that my illnesses did not define me. Rheumatoid Arthritis, Fibromyalgia, and anxiety were parts of my life, but they were not my identity. I was more than my diagnosis. This realization was liberating. It allowed me to embrace my journey with a new perspective, one that focused on thriving rather than merely surviving.

The experience of battling illness and confronting my mortality had transformed me. I emerged from the hospital with a renewed sense of purpose. I had an awakening within and became truly present in my life, realizing I am more than any limitations or labels. I knew that I had to share my journey with others, to help them see that they, too, could overcome their challenges and live fulfilling lives despite their illnesses or any barriers, fears, or overwhelming circumstances standing in their way. I wanted to help others discover and embrace the fact that they are made for more.

My background as a Registered Nurse provided a solid foundation for this new path. I decided to become a Board-Certified Transformational Life Coach, empowering others to conquer their fears and rise above their challenges. My goal was to help others live well with their illnesses or any obstacles they faced. I wanted to show them that they could make positive changes, improve their health, and live fulfilling lives. The process of becoming a life coach was both challenging and rewarding. I immersed myself in studies, learning the skills and techniques needed to support others effectively. I drew on my personal experiences and professional background to develop a coaching practice that was empathetic, compassionate, knowledgeable, and transformative.

Today, I am dedicated to impacting the lives of others. Through my coaching practice, I work with individuals facing various health and life challenges, helping them navigate their journeys with resilience and hope. I provide guidance on holistic health practices, mindfulness, and lifestyle changes that support their overall well-being. Each client I work with is a reminder of the importance of this work. Seeing them make positive changes, overcome obstacles, and thrive despite their challenges is incredibly fulfilling. It reinforces my belief that we are not defined by our illnesses or limitations. We have the power to create lives filled with purpose, joy, love, and health.

Reflecting on my journey, I am filled with gratitude. The daunting experience in the hospital was a turning point that led to a profound personal transformation. It taught me the importance of holistic health, self-care, self-love, and resilience. It showed me that while we cannot control everything, we have the power to make choices that support our well-being.

I am not defined by my illnesses but by my strength, resilience, and unwavering spirit. I face each day with the knowledge that I can overcome whatever challenges come my way. My journey has been one of survival, transformation, and empowerment, and I am proud of the person I have become. Looking forward, I am committed to continuing my holistic approach to health and well-being. I will keep exploring new ways to support my body and mind, staying open to learning and growth. I will cherish my relationships, nurturing the bonds that have sustained me through my darkest times.

The journey towards health and wellness is ongoing. I continue to learn, grow, and adapt, like the sun's rays spreading across the horizon, illuminating new paths and opportunities each day. Each day brings new challenges and opportunities for growth. I remain committed to my holistic lifestyle, constantly seeking ways to enhance my well-being and support my immune system. I also remain dedicated to my clients, helping them navigate their journeys with compassion and expertise. Their successes are my successes, and their struggles remind me of the importance of the work we do together. Through my coaching, I aim to inspire, empower, and uplift, helping others see that they too can live well despite their challenges.

My life is now filled with purpose and meaning. The experience of facing my mortality and emerging stronger has given me a profound appreciation for life. I am grateful for the opportunity to help others and to make a difference in their lives.

Emerging from the hospital was like stepping into a new world. The first breath of fresh air felt like a victory. I was weak, but the sunlight on my skin gave me a sense of hope and renewal. As I walked out, supported by my family, I vowed to take every step necessary to rebuild my strength and health. The first few weeks at home were challenging. Simple tasks like getting out of bed or preparing a meal or going to the mailbox exhausted me. I had to pace myself, taking frequent breaks and being patient with my body's slow recovery. It was frustrating at times, but I reminded myself that every small step was progress.

I created a structured daily routine to aid my recovery. Mornings started with gentle stretching exercises to wake up my muscles and joints. I incorporated breathing exercises to improve my lung capacity and reduce anxiety. My daughters helped me prepare healthy meals, ensuring I received all the vitamins and minerals needed to support my healing process. Although I was physically isolated, the support from my community was unwavering. Friends and family reached out regularly through phone calls, video chats, and messages. Their words of encouragement were like a soft blanket on a cold dreary night. Once, a few of my friends arrived in their cars at my house, bearing a banner and singing "Happy Birthday" to me. They played drum sounds with pots and spoons, honking their horns, and waving as they circled in my driveway as they could not approach closer due to my weakened immune system, warming my heart and making me feel deeply connected, loved, and supported.

One of the most significant sources of support came from online groups dedicated to individuals living with chronic illnesses. I found comfort in connecting with others who understood my struggles. We shared our experiences and coping strategies, and celebrated each other's victories, no matter how small. These connections were invaluable, reminding me that I was not alone in my journey.

As my strength gradually returned, I began to rediscover the activities that brought me joy. Gardening, a hobby I had abandoned due to my illnesses, became a therapeutic practice. Tending to plants, feeling the soil in my hands, and watching new flowers grow was incredibly healing. It was a reminder of the resilience of life and the potential for growth even in the most challenging conditions. I also rekindled my love for dance and music. Just dancing freely and listening to music, even for a few minutes each day, lifted my spirits and provided a creative outlet for my emotions. Music became a form of meditation, helping me to relax and stay present, like a soft breeze soothing my mind and clearing away the noise and clutter. Dancing freely became a safe haven where I could be my true self, like finding shelter under an umbrella in a sudden downpour. It shields me from judgment and allows me to express my emotions openly and authentically, creating a space of comfort and acceptance. These moments of joy were crucial in balancing the physical and emotional demands of my recovery.

My journey towards health and wellness was not just about physical recovery; it was also a journey of learning and personal growth for my emotional and mental well-being. I immersed myself in books, articles, and online courses on holistic health, nutrition, wellness, and mindset. The more I learned, the more empowered I felt to make informed decisions about my health.

I discovered the benefits of healthy eating of whole plant-based foods and supplements that supported my immune system and helped manage the symptoms of Rheumatoid Arthritis and Fibromyalgia. The results were promising, with noticeable improvements in my energy levels and pain management. I also explored the mind-body connection, understanding how stress and emotions impacted my physical health. The body really does speak to us if we just take the time to listen and always be kind to ourselves. Techniques such as guided imagery, yoga, journaling, prayer, and deep breathing exercises became part of my toolkit for managing anxiety and promoting overall well-being. These practices taught me to listen to my body and respond with compassion and care.

One of the most profound lessons I learned was the importance of resilience. My experience in the hospital had tested my limits, but it also revealed a deep source of inner strength I hadn't known I possessed. Building resilience became a central theme in my recovery. I focused on setting realistic goals and celebrating small achievements. Each day, I acknowledged my progress, whether it was walking a little farther, cooking a nutritious meal, or completing a meditation session. These victories, no matter how minor they seemed, were milestones on my journey. I also learned to reframe setbacks as opportunities for growth. Instead of viewing bad days as failures, I saw them as reminders to be kind to myself and to adjust my approach. This mindset shift was crucial in maintaining a positive outlook and staying motivated.

As my health improved, I felt a growing desire to share my journey and inspire others. I started sharing my experiences and the strategies that had helped me. Speaking about this on Zoom calls became a therapeutic practice allowing me to reflect on my journey and connect with a wider audience. I shared my tips on holistic health I was implementing, exercise routines, and mindfulness practices. I connected with others who found hope and encouragement in my story. These sessions provided a platform for people to share their stories, ask questions, and support each other. The sense of community and shared purpose was incredibly powerful. Together, we celebrated our success, navigated our setbacks, and grew stronger. Knowing that my experiences could help others made the challenges I had faced feel meaningful and worthwhile.

My journey of transformation led me to a new career path. Becoming a Board-Certified Life Coach was a natural progression, combining my nursing background with my passion for holistic health and personal development. I enrolled in a comprehensive training program, learning coaching techniques, psychology, and business skills. It was Robbins Madanes' Training Center and the prestigious school where Tony Robbins and Chloe Madanes taught. The training was intense, but it was also deeply rewarding. I developed the skills to guide others through their challenges, helping them set goals, overcome obstacles, and achieve their full potential. My personal experience added depth and empathy to my coaching practice, allowing me to connect with clients on a profound level.

Today, as a Transformational Life Coach, I am dedicated to empowering others to live their best lives. I work with clients facing chronic illnesses, and other life challenges helping them develop holistic health plans, manage stress, and build resilience. My approach is client-centered, focusing on their unique needs and goals. These sessions provide practical tools and strategies that my clients can integrate into their daily lives. Seeing the positive impact of my work on others is incredibly fulfilling and reinforces my commitment to this path.

One of the most rewarding aspects of my work is witnessing my clients' transformations. Their journeys are a testament to the power of resilience, determination, and holistic health practices. Each success story is a reminder that we all have the potential to overcome challenges and thrive.

My journey towards health and wellness is ongoing. I continue to learn, grow, and adapt, embracing new practices and insights that support my well-being. I remain committed to a holistic lifestyle, constantly seeking ways to enhance my health and balance my life. I also continue to share my story, hoping to inspire others to take charge of their health and well-being. Through my coaching practice, speaking events, and workshops, I aim to create a ripple effect, empowering others to make positive changes in their lives.

Living with chronic illnesses will always be a part of my reality, but it does not define me. I am defined by my strength, resilience, and the choices I make to support my health and happiness. I am grateful for the journey, with all its challenges and triumphs, as it has shaped me into the person I am today. As I reflect on my journey, I am filled with gratitude. The experience of facing my mortality and emerging stronger has given me a profound appreciation for life. I am grateful for the support of my family, friends, and community, who stood by me during my darkest times.

I am also grateful for the lessons I have learned and the growth I have experienced. Each challenge has been an opportunity to build resilience, learn, and evolve. I am proud of the progress I have made and the person I have become.

Looking forward, I am excited about the future. I am committed to continuing my holistic approach to health and well-being, exploring new ways to support my body and mind. I am dedicated to my clients, helping them navigate their journeys with compassion and expertise. The future is filled with possibilities. I am excited to continue my journey, embracing new challenges and opportunities for growth. I remain committed to my health, well-being, and the work I do to empower others. I will continue to learn, adapt, and grow, always seeking ways to enhance my holistic lifestyle. I will cherish my relationships, nurturing the bonds that have sustained me through my darkest times. I will live each day with gratitude, knowing that I have the strength and resilience to overcome whatever challenges come my way.

My journey is a testament to the power of resilience, determination, and holistic health practices. It is a reminder that we are not defined by our illnesses or limitations but by our strength, courage, and the choices we make. I am grateful for the journey, with all its challenges and triumphs, as it has shaped me into the person I am today.

One of the most rewarding aspects of my journey has been witnessing the ripple effect of my work. The clients I have coached, and others that I have interacted with on different platforms, have all made positive changes in their lives. They have embraced holistic health practices, built resilience, and found new strength in the face of challenges. Seeing their transformations is incredibly fulfilling. It reinforces my belief in the power of holistic health and the importance of taking charge of our well-being. Each success story is a testament to the potential we all must overcome obstacles and thrive, not just survive. As I continue my journey, I am committed to expanding my reach and impact. I will continue to share my story, offer support, and provide guidance to those in need. Like a lighthouse guiding ships through turbulent waters, I aim to illuminate paths of self-discovery and empowerment. Just as my own awakening within has transformed me, I am dedicated to nurturing the light within each individual, helping them navigate life's challenges, embrace their true potential, and live authentically.

Raffy Sgroi

Sage Advice
Business Development Director

https://au.linkedin.com/in/raffy-sgroi-pcc-maicd-bcom-2a349b11b
https://fempire.com.au/places/raffy-sgroi/
https://www.instagram.com/raffy_sgroi/
https://sageadvice.au/
https://zestcanberra.com.au/
https://carmechanicalservices.com.au/

Raffy Sgroi, originally from Milan, moved Down Under in 2001. With a Bachelor of Commerce background, she is a speaker and an international multi-award-winning nine-figure entrepreneur with over 20 years of experience in the business scene. She is a professional master of business and career consultant. Raffy is a champion for inclusive and sustainable workplaces, firmly believing in the power of diversity and gender equality. She is a proud mother of two incredible human beings, Francesco and Agatha, and the blessed wife of her life & business partner, Charlie. In the Capital Territory, Raffy is well-known for her advocacy for inclusive and diverse workplaces and her unwavering commitment to sustainability.

Three, two, one. Reset

By Raffy Sgroi

Is it possible to reset one's life and start over from scratch? Are there age limits beyond which it is impossible to do so? And what does it mean to start over and turn the page? I want to talk about this because it's a question I am often asked. As usual, the answer is hidden in the question. The only thing left to understand is whether this answer that people like you usually give (most of the time, "no, it's impossible, it's too complicated") is only possible.

Many people dream of starting over from scratch. Behind this desire, which touches the boundaries of aspiration, is often a feeling of dissatisfaction with one's life combined with the growing frustration of being unable to change it.

From my interactions in my professional experience, I have come to believe that the desire to start over often corresponds to an attempt to immediately erase, with a vigorous sweep, the effects of a great disappointment. Not everyone wants to start over from scratch. Through a wise operation of reasoning, some wonder where to start again and what to change. But it is never easy.

Without thinking twice - The other profession of living

Women lie; they always lie at all costs. Lie to avoid confrontation, lie to protect who they love, lie to claim what they deserve in a world that never sees them, lie to see their children's happiness, lie to please, lie to forget, lie to survive. And there's no wonder: they have lies in their very genitals. Who will ever know when a woman has enjoyed it?

So there I was, staring out of the airplane window, heart pounding like a drum solo. I'd left the charming, twisty streets of Italy behind for the wild unknown of Australia. "Great idea," I muttered, remembering why I thought this was a good plan. With excitement and sheer panic, I promised myself, "I'm going to make it here, no matter what." Right?...!

In 2001, I said Arrivederci Milan with nothing but my stubbornness, two English words—hello, thank you a164 Australian Dollars and thirty cents and a useless Bachelor's Degree. Leaving the comfort of home wasn't exactly a walk in the park, but I was hungry for something new.

When the plane landed in Sydney, my heart was about to explode. The airport was a noisy mess of different languages, reminding me how out of place I was. The first days were anything but glamorous. With my lousy English, I quickly realized this would be harder than I thought. But was I giving up? That was not my style. I rolled up my sleeves and got to work.

My grand adventure started at the bottom, washing dishes in a tiny restaurant. Hot water, soap suds, and sore hands became my new best friends. Each dish I scrubbed was a small step toward my goal. I had a vision, and I was willing to work my butt off to get there.

Weeks have turned into months. My stubbornness paid off. I soaked up every knowledge I could from my job and coworkers. Slowly, adding extra words to my new dictionary, and so did my confidence.

My relentless spirit caught the eye of the local Italian community in Sydney. My Aunt Pina was my biggest cheerleader. She welcomed me with open arms and heart, giving me a sense of belonging that was a lifesaver during those lonely, homesick days.

Pina and her husband, Zio Raffaele, were more than family; they guided me in this crazy new chapter. They introduced me to the lively Italian community in Sydney, where I found a piece of home. Through shared meals, stories, and traditions, I started to feel a bit more settled.

Their constant support was my lifeline, helping me grow in ways I never imagined. With their encouragement, I climbed the ladder, moving from dishwashing to better roles in the hospitality industry. As my skills grew, so did my opportunities.

Looking back, I can't help but laugh. My challenges made me a woman of strength, resilience, and endless gratitude. I've come a long way from a clueless immigrant with a dream.

This first chapter of my story is about courage, stubbornness, and the unwavering support of family and community. And guess what? This was just the beginning of a wild ride that would leave a mark on me and my new home.

It's raining, and it's time to learn to dance in the rain.

Life has a way of throwing curveballs when you least expect them. But if there's one thing I've learned on this incredible journey, the secret to a fulfilling life isn't about avoiding the storms but learning to dance in the rain.

I remember a stormy afternoon in Sydney shortly after I started working at the pasta shop. The sky was a moody shade of gray, and the downpour was relentless. The kind of rain made you want to curl up with a good book and a cup of tea. But life doesn't always give you the luxury of choosing comfort over duty. I had a shift to cover, and the pasta shop didn't close for anything as trivial as bad weather.

As I dashed from one awning to another, trying to avoid getting completely soaked, I couldn't help but laugh at the absurdity of it all. Here I was, a young woman from Italy, navigating the streets of Sydney in a torrential downpour, chasing a dream that seemed as elusive as a rainbow. After all, Australia is the land of endless summer in the movies. But in that moment, I felt a surge of empowerment. I was living my life, embracing every challenge, and finding joy in the journey.

When I finally arrived at the shop, drenched but smiling, the owner greeted me with a warm chuckle. "You look like you've been swimming!" he exclaimed, handing me a towel. As I dried off and prepared for my shift, I realized something profound: life is messy, unpredictable, and often challenging, but it's also beautiful, rewarding, and full of unexpected joys.

That rainy day became a metaphor for my life. It taught me that no matter what obstacles come your way, you have the power to face them head-on and emerge more robust and more resilient. As I continued to navigate my journey, I discovered that this mindset wasn't just about surviving—it was about thriving. Trust me, my weather forecast always includes a chance of rain and a possibility of a tsunami. Stay vigilant!

"Embrace the unexpected, for it's often where the magic happens. Surround yourself with your tribe—those who lift you, cheer you on, and remind you that you can weather any storm together."

One of the most empowering lessons I've learned is the importance of embracing the unexpected. Life rarely goes according to plan, and that's okay. Some of the most beautiful moments come from the unplanned, the spontaneous, and the unexpected detours.

It's crucial to find your tribe. Surround yourself with people who uplift you, support you, and inspire you to be the best version of yourself. For me, my tribe included my family, the Italian community, and my professional sisterhood.

These relationships gave me a sense of belonging and an invaluable support system. They reminded me that I wasn't alone in my journey and that we could overcome any challenge together.

Life is too short to settle for anything less than what sets your soul on fire. Pursue your passion with all your heart, and don't let fear or doubt hold you back. For me, that passion was to empower incredible young women and create a legacy for my girl, my daughter Agatha.

Life is too short to settle for anything less than what sets your soul on fire. So, go ahead and chase your passion with everything you've got! Don't let fear or doubt stand in your way—they're just speed bumps on the road to your dreams. For me, that passion was all about empowering incredible young women and creating a legacy for my fantastic daughter, Agatha. Whether through mentoring, storytelling, or simply leading by example, I'm all in. Because when you pursue what you love, not only do you light up your own life, but you also become a beacon for others. So, grab that passion by the horns and ride it to your dreams!

"Celebrating Your Journey"

As women, we often downplay our achievements and focus on what we haven't accomplished. But it's essential to celebrate your journey and recognize how far you've come. Every step, no matter how small, is a victory. Fastforward a few years from that Italian dreamer, and I met an incredible soul, Charlie. My rock, my business partner, is the reason behind my success: a mother and a fresh small business owner. Charlie and I weathered rain, storms, and tsunamis—from full-time caring for his brother with Down syndrome, starting our Automotive business, and navigating the challenges of a premature baby to raising two kids and facing my cancer diagnosis. Skip 364 chapters, and here I am, still married to this incredible man who never surprises me. I am the proud mother of a nearly 15-year-old, very handsome young man, Francesco, and a 13-year-old going on 25, young woman, Agatha. I'm an international award-winning nine-figure entrepreneur, mentor, advocate for inclusion and diversity, master business and career consultant, and co-writer of this incredible book. Celebrating this journey is about acknowledging the milestones and honoring the resilience, love, and relentless spirit that got me here.

One of the most fulfilling aspects of my journey has been the opportunity to empower others. Whether mentoring young women, supporting fellow immigrants, or simply sharing my story, I strive to inspire others to pursue their dreams and embrace their unique journey.

Life is a precious gift, and we have one chance to make the most of it. So, to all the incredible women out there: embrace your journey, dance in the rain, and pursue your dreams with all your heart. You can create a unique life filled with joy, passion, and endless possibilities.

And there you have it, Sisters, from washing dishes to becoming a nine-figure entrepreneur and co-authoring this book while dodging life's curveballs like a pro. If I can survive premature babies, cancer, and Charlie's questionable taste in loud cars, then you, too, can conquer your roller coaster of a journey. And let's be honest—if women can lie about loving their husband's terrible taste in gifts to keep the peace, we can handle anything life throws our way. So, here's to chase dreams, celebrating every tiny victory, and laughing in the face of adversity—because if we can't laugh, we might as well cry into our overpriced lattes. Cheers to the wild ride that is life!

Kimberly Mihalik-Blackstone

Co-Founder and CEO of KSB creative Solutions &
Clear To Close Solutions

https://www.linkedin.com/in/kimberly-mihalik-8b468723b/
https://www.facebook.com/kimberly.mihalik
https://www.instagram.com/pivotwithpurpose.kim
http://www.ksbsolutions.net/

Kimberly is a dynamic Nursepreneur with 31 years of healthcare experience, 22 years as a nurse in multiple roles & settings. She is also a real estate investor that specializes in solving complex problems with advanced real estate strategies utilizing creative solutions. Kim is also an Author, live weekly podcast host, Key note speaker, CPR Instructor, Consultant & Coach, CEO of Mihalik Mountain Ministry in honor of fallen State Trooper Robert J Mihalik who was murdered in the line of duty, MAP-SCDY member, endurance athlete for a decade, Zebra warrior =(Ehlers-Danlos Syndrome & Lupus) & the most important role~ Mother to two terrific teenage boys. The state shaped like a mitten mirrors her love with the outdoors, beaches, 4 seasons & mayberry like towns~summers are pure midwest magic up & down the coast! Kimberly is looking forward to chasing the weather within 5 years, until then she scoots around in her RV creating memories of the present.

Pressure is a Privilege ~ Pivot with Purpose!

By Kimberly Mihalik-Blackstone

Let's go on a journey as I share my narrative of persevering and pivoting with purpose to propel the kingdom of God. It is magical, messy, and marked by lessons learned from every experience with each step molding me into the person I am today. I invite you to view the world through my vision to experience the intricate and intimate seasons that have shaped my existence. Words of wisdom aren't always whimsical, polished, or eloquent. Sometimes they're single short sentences summed up and muttered by a training partner, "Kim, you're really good at suffering, you'll be fine." That one-liner was proudly received on a tough training day during a hot, humid summer day. Endurance racing helped transform my life in countless ways. The grueling nature of long distances demanded physical stamina and mental fortitude, pushing me to confront and overcome my limits. The journey you will read about instilled a sense of discipline and time management as I balanced rigorous training schedules with daily responsibilities. It also introduced me to a community of like-minded individuals who inspired and supported each other, fostering a sense of camaraderie and belonging. The perseverance you need to beat the odds has helped me in my newest chapter of life, the 3 D's: death, divorce, and diagnosis. The death of my DNA contributor & precious dog Sheena, the diagnosis of a genetic condition, and a divorce after 2 decades. Stamina in endurance racing is crucial, in many ways, a race consisting of 70.3 miles of swimming (1.2 mile swim, 56 mile bike and 13.1 mile run) mimics life in its rawest form. It's the mullet version of all things questionable, business up front with the party in the back not knowing which style of swagger to sport. Back of the packers (aka me) in an endurance race is one of the most unique experiences you will ever partake in. Triathlon has saved my life in more ways than one. The journey to get to that start line at an Ironman race is a trek of countless hours of discipline and internal personal dialogues. If Jesus had given me cliff notes of what my life would look like pushing fifty I would have chuckled so hard and said sure boss!

I have had many seasons of suffering where the storms were so tsunami-like that you can only find solace and strength in scripture without drowning in the depths of despair. I was born and raised in a state shaped like a Mitten (Michigan) outside Detroit—Motor city style sandwiched between the baby boomers and millennials. I am a Gen Xer; we are known for resilience and adaptability, and have debate classes in elementary. We learned how to respectfully agree to disagree or use our fists to decide who the superior was, a pecking order that was very efficient in my lower middle-class hood. Growing up during a time of significant cultural and technology shifts I witnessed the rise of a globalizing world. I can't declare that I have always been the most tolerant in turbulent times. Exiting a childhood home in your early teenage years as a feral couch surfer led to unhealthy coping mechanisms throughout young adulthood. The choices I made along the way with my shrunken hippocampus and dysregulated amygdala set me up for future quagmires. Statistically speaking, hurt people tend to hurt people, but I was a healer instead.

Culturally, Gen Xers are often associated with diversity and known for their skepticism towards authority and institutions, a trait forged in part by witnessing economic downturns, political scandals, and shifting societal norms during their formative years. We continue to make a significant impact on society with our distinctive blend of pragmatism, resourcefulness, and a penchant for questioning the status quo. SO… It shouldn't be shocking that I started my entrepreneurship journey after finishing my third half Ironman on my 46th birthday with EDS (Ehlers-Danlos syndrome). I wasn't always endurance Ironman fit, I have struggled with my weight and self-worth most of my life. My childhood was filled with moments of insecurity, abuse, and self-doubt especially when it came to body image. Sexual, physical, and mental abuse rendered me to a coping mechanism of turning to food. Since my first weight loss story was published, I have kept a healthy weight naturally for a decade—no gimmicks, meds, surgery, just pure vanilla consistency, grit, and healthier strategies. Nearly 100 pounds of baggage was lost for good. It wasn't just the weight I lost, but everything that was wrapped within my fascia holding me hostage.

Much like endurance racing, entrepreneurship is an amazing art form that is complex, creative, and oftentimes, complete chaos. These pioneers, like athletes, usually are innovators with enormous goals. Typically these creatures are driven by passion, philanthropy, and profit combined with a desire to make a meaningful impact in the world. The journey is often marked by uncertainty and risk but also by creativity, resilience, and tenacity. Networking with like-minded individuals revealed a pattern of highly driven powerhouses and oftentimes, these humans have a humbling story of pushing through many adversities. This narrow path provides a culture of growth and adaptability within their circle. Navigating the complexities of different demands while staying true to their vision is challenging, to say the least. Success on this route can't be measured by financial gain, but rather by the ability to solve a problem creatively while inspiring and building others up along the way. I was the happy helper leader in many of the roles that I have held throughout my 49 years on this earth. When asked the common question of what I do for a living, I fumble on that description but can relate to the chameleon. Chameleons are known for the ability to adapt and change with their environment which is crucial in everything I have accomplished in my 49 years. As a nurse, I worked in high-stress environments like the ICU/CTICU and always thrived in the chaos. Now that I understand neuroscience better, my stormy seasons have given me the capability of keeping calm in high-pressure environments. Exit strategies, resourcefulness, and perseverance are all qualities needed for endurance, athletes, motherhood, nursing, or entrepreneurship. Essentially, I have two sides. My real estate investing alter ego and an entrepreneur that combines nursing and equals to a Nursepreneur. On the real estate side, I close on buy and hold single-family homes and consult on projects like residential assisted living, sober living, short-term rentals, private money lending and partnering. I am a natural connector of all things resources and take pleasure in scaling not only myself but also others. I talk about real estate investing as a podcast host live at 5 every Tuesday for the Pace Morby media team. My Nursepreneur side is my favorite—I have been a nurse for 22 years and in healthcare for 32. Although real estate investing and consulting are my main income, it acts as a vehicle so I can combine my love of nursing and nurturing to combine passion and profit.

I am also an author, keynote speaker, wellness and life coach, and CPR instructor, and I have a ministry in honor of my kids' grandpa who was murdered in the line of duty as a state trooper. Mihalik Mountain Ministry has impacted so many local families. Internationally, the ministry has helped kids, clinics, schools, and safe water resources. One of my many missions in life is to get information about EDS (Ehlers-Danlos syndrome). It took two decades to diagnose and current research states it isn't rare, but rather misdiagnosed. It can be a debilitating condition that leaves many people disabled. I continue to control how I respond to an overwhelming incurable genetic diagnosis and not be a victim. As I continue to struggle with the complications from EDS, every finish line and accomplishment is more meaningful.

Obstacles will always be present and continue to suck the blood out of your body like a pestering tick if you can't pivot with purpose. Like a tick, the aftermath of the bite can leave disease or death from the parasite that was presented with an opportunity. The 3 lbs of jelly that lies within your skull controls your functionality from your nervous system to your mindset. This can catapult you into a negative or positive spiral with simple neuro hacks that can help you sink or swim. Unlike symbiotic relationships, parasites that are disguised as people or addiction will continue to control a good majority of the talents and tools available to pull yourself out of the pit. Unlike a salmon who chose to swim upstream to lay their eggs and die, most people aren't willing to sacrifice their vices to propel themselves into a positive middle ground. Our flesh will continue to rot if we don't solve problems innovatively and harvest the goodness that was already within us when we formed in our mother's womb. Many times we just need an experience, season, or a storm to unleash the warrior that has been swept aside. The people you meet and the experiences you have are for a reason, season lesson, or lifetime. Perspective versus perception, it's often perplexing to view the world to understand not respond to it. The old cliche coaching verbiage of "you can only control how you respond" is like a Richard Simmons' hack, an oldie but a goodie. Different variables will forever be a part of the equation most folks lack to have the emotional intelligence to be self-reflective and refine their situations to suffer through the storm with their eyes fixed upon Jesus.

Striving to avoid mediocrity is embracing the excellence God gave you and pushing beyond average. It involves long days and setting high standards for oneself and continuously seeking improvements in all areas of your life. Being exceptional requires sacrifices, dedication, and a commitment to lifelong learning. It means not settling but rather aiming for greatness in every endeavor. This type of determination fosters innovation, creativity, and resilience, enabling folks to stand out and make a significant impact. It leads to personal growth, emotional intelligence, fulfillment, and the ability to inspire and influence others positively. Suffering is a profound and harrowing experience that tests the limits of human endurance and character.

For many reading this, it comes in various forms, whether it is due to race, religion, political beliefs, or social status. It often involves systematic oppression, discrimination, and physical, emotional, or sexual abuse. Those who have suffered persecution are frequently marginalized, stripped of their rights, and live in fear. This can lead to deep scarring that can and will stop you from doing great things God had planned for you. The psychological toll can be immense, leading to feelings of isolation, hopelessness, and despair. Despite the immense hardships, many who endure this demonstrate extraordinary courage and strength in many forms. This resilience is a testament to the human's spirit capacity to withstand severe adversity. In the face of oppression and healing these individuals often find solidarity within their network and draw strength from their convictions and beliefs. This very personal fight against tyranny has historically led to significant social and political changes who have the courage to stand against injustice. These internal struggles highlight the urgent need for global awareness, advocacy, and action to uphold human rights for the most vulnerable people.

In whatever season you are in, ride the route of uncertainty with powerful reminders in scripture knowing God will guide and mold your life. Equip yourself with scripture whatever season you're in and go confident, spreading the word of the Lord amongst the earth. Telling your story is a powerful act of self-expression and connection. It allows you to share your unique experiences, perspectives, and lessons learned fostering empathy and understanding. When you narrate your journey, you give your voice to your triumphs and struggles helping others see the world through your eyes. This act of storytelling can be cathartic offering a sense of healing through words. It also has the potential to inspire and motivate others in similar situations. By telling my story, I can contribute to a collective tapestry of human experience, reminding everyone on earth they are not alone in their journey. My prayer for those reading my cliff note version: embrace the persecution, pivot with purpose, and remind yourself that pressure is a privilege and mediocrity is a choice. Shalom!!!! SHAZAM!!!

Helen M Gaines

CEO of HMG Services and Solutions LLC

https://www.linkedin.com/in/helenmgaines
https://facebook.com/helenparkergaines
https://www.instagram.com/drhelengaines/
http://helenmkennedy.com
https://helenmkennedy.info

Helen M. Gaines is a distinguished religious leader, founder of several Christian organizations, a serial entrepreneur, and honorary doctorate recipient in Christian Theology. An esteemed family matriarch—mother of six, grandmother of sixteen, and great-grandmother of two—she began her pastoral journey in 2000 and currently leads Sanctuary of Living Waters and co-pastors Anointed By Christ International Christian Center with her husband, Dr. Johnny Gaines. Helen founded The Community Empowerment Organization and the Morning Glory Devotional and Radio Hour, collaborating with Life in The Word Radio Broadcast. An accomplished author, her works include "He Heals the Brokenhearted," "The Best Life is a Grateful Life," and "31 Days of Encouragement, Inspiration, and Affirmations for Cancer Warriors." She's currently writing "A Walk Thru the Valley" about overcoming pancreatic cancer, which inspired the Caring Hearts and Hands Cancer Care Ministry. Helen's message of faith and empowerment continues to impact many lives.

A Walk Thru the Valley—
My Journey of Grace

By Helen M Gaines

"Yes, though I walk through the [deep, sunless] valley of the shadow of death, I will fear or dread no evil, for You are with me; Your rod [to protect] and Your staff [to guide], they comfort me."
Psalm 23:4 Amplified Version

Our lives are similar to a quilt woven of unique patterns of joys and sorrows, highs and lows, mountaintops and valleys. When completed, the coverlet tells the story of a life traveled. It was June 18, 1980 that I began a new life's path journeying through the sacred scriptures which have served as a guiding light, illuminating my pathway through peaceful and stormy times. The entirety of the scriptures has offered comfort and strength, shaping my perspective on the trials and triumphs that life presents. Among the revered texts, Job's story, found in the 18th book of the Bible, has been the impetus that's helped me endure the sundries of shadows in the tapestry of my life.

Job's journey, besieged with crushing losses and intense suffering, included the murder of his servants, the theft of his livestock, and the tragic loss of his children caused by a natural disaster. His physical body endured extreme pain and suffering, while his closest companion, Mrs. Job (not named in scriptures), suggested he *"curse God and die"* (Job 2:9 KJV). The friends he relied on for comfort judged him instead, insinuating that his calamity resulted from his wrongdoing. Yet, amidst this downpour of adversity, Job's response was an example of steadfast faith: *"The Lord gives, and the Lord takes away"* (Job 1:21b). His unwavering resolve amidst despair was a potent reminder during my ordeal with cancer. Standing on the precipice of my cancer diagnosis, I clung to the same unshakeable faith as Job. God revealed His grace through His word, which prepared me spiritually, mentally, and emotionally to embark on this journey courageously while walking through my valley of the shadow of death.

When the doctor initially uttered those life-altering words, "You have pancreatic cancer," a thousand thoughts flooded my mind. Not, *"How long will I live?"* But *"How would I tell my family?" "How would this alter all my plans?"* At that moment, my life became shrouded in darkness, and suddenly, it changed. I would face challenges that would test the very core of my being and belief system. But while I navigated through this valley, bombarded at times by fear, confusion, and disbelief at varying degrees, I discovered depths of strength, hope, and faith I never knew I possessed.

Here begins a chapter in my story—a patch in my quilt, a testimony of the sacred journey that shaped and strengthened me, a walk through the valley of cancer where I found more than survival; I found grace.

My cancer journey began in the middle of June 2023. Less than two years prior, and after 17 years of widowhood, I married a wonderful man, a ministry partner, and best friend. We were just coming out of our honeymoon phase. We both served as lead pastors of two ministries and were extremely excited about the respective ministries' direction. It was a busy time as we were preparing for four weeks of events during July, which would commence with the celebration of his 16th church and pastoral anniversary, my birthday celebration, and three weeks of travel for both ministry work and personal reasons.

Feeling revitalized from shedding a few pounds—following a 6-week weight loss program that included a change in diet, exercise, and weekly injections, I began to experience persistent abdominal discomfort, loss of appetite, and nausea. Initially, I attributed the gnawing pain to the recent dietary changes. However, when over-the-counter antacids failed to provide relief, I realized the problem might be more complex.

The pain intensified and traveled to the right side of my abdomen before moving into the center of my back. At first, I wondered if I was trying to pass a kidney stone, a condition I had experienced before. I purchased an over-the-counter urine test to determine if blood was in my urine, but the result was negative. There were other symptoms I initially shrugged off: my urine had darkened and my bowel movements were unusually pale, almost white. Little did I know that these were signs of pancreatic cancer.

Night after night, the pain worsened, and nothing brought relief except lying on my stomach with my knees drawn up to my chest. Of course, I couldn't sleep in this posture throughout the night when I did sleep, and sitting or reclining did nothing to alleviate the discomfort. I began to fear eating because this exacerbated the pain as well. My husband suggested I go to the emergency room, but I declined, replying, *"I'm waiting for God to give me direction."* I tried to hide the degree of discomfort I felt from him, but he often overheard me moaning while trying to rest. Driven by concern about the persistent pain I was experiencing, he fervently petitioned God in prayer to reveal anything hidden that was causing my distress. His prayer request moved me so deeply that I now felt the seriousness of my condition.

God's answers to our prayers can happen in subtle ways. A few days after my husband's prayer, while finalizing my schedule with my assistant, I told her, *"I'm going to Holy Cross Hospital to get checked out."* My husband interrupted my phone conversation, asking when I had made that decision, to which I replied, *"I didn't. It just came out of my mouth."* In other words, I had not contemplated it before that moment, realizing I had never stepped foot in that hospital in my five decades of living in Fort Lauderdale. I tried to circumvent the unction by settling for an urgent care center, but the impression was too strong – *"Go to the ER!"* Two days later I found myself at Holy Cross Hospital, led by a sense of urgency from Holy Spirit.

That first ER visit at Holy Cross Hospital was on July 2nd. When I shared my physical history with the ER physician, the usual tests—blood work, urinalysis, chest X-ray, and ultrasound—were ordered. The ultrasound technician ominously noted that my gallbladder was *"not happy."* The ER physician returned and determinedly questioned me about alcohol consumption, recreational drug use, or any other prescription or OTC medications I might have recently taken. Besides the weight loss medication, I had only been taking an all-natural detox vitamin. When reviewing its contents, the physician reported that it was not causing my issue. She advised me that my urinalysis was negative for blood, and my X-ray and ultrasound were negative for kidney stones. However, I did have an elevated liver function test (LFT) and bile was in my urine (bilirubinuria). She further informed me that she was admitting me for further evaluation and a cholecystectomy (gallbladder removal). I had not considered an overnight stay or surgery as an outcome. I believed I would go in, get the necessary labs done, receive a prescription, and go home.

It would be five hours before a room was ready for me. Confined to the frigid emergency room, I repeatedly watched the marquee on the computer screen before I noticed the hospital's mission statement: *"We, Holy Cross Hospital and Trinity Health, serve together **in the spirit of the Gospel** as a compassionate and transforming healing presence within our communities."* The phrase *"in the spirit of the Gospel"* confirmed that God had led me there, and I felt safe in His arms and loving care. I proceeded to ask each hospital employee who walked into my room—physicians, technicians, nurses, environmental services staff, transporters, and the admitting clerk—if they knew the hospital's mission statement. Not one of them knew it verbatim, however, they all demonstrated compassion, and there was a palpable healing presence in that place. That presence was Jehovah-Rapha.

Finally arriving in my room at around 7:30 that evening, I was exhausted and hungry. The kitchen was closed but the nursing assistant offered me a cold sandwich and a container of apple juice. After my husband's departure, I went to sleep—too exhausted to be bothered by all that had transpired that day.

The following morning I had breakfast because no orders indicated I should be NPO (nothing by mouth). I briefly spoke with my son, Reginald, who is an interventional radiology technician who had undergone a cholecystectomy himself. He assured me it was a routine procedure, and with the new techniques, I should be out in a day or two without having to disrupt my travel plans.

Just after noon, the "on-call" gastroenterologist hurriedly entered my room. Learning that I had eaten breakfast and not enough time had elapsed for him to perform an ERCP (endoscopic retrograde cholangiopancreatography)—a procedure to place a stent to open up the obstruction found in the duct between my liver, gallbladder, and pancreas to allow the bile to flow—, he became upset and appeared anxious. This news was too much for me to digest. He suggested that due to the holiday (the 4th of July) and low staffing, I should remain in the hospital for the procedure to be performed two days later, on that Thursday morning, since I was already admitted. In doing so, I would prevent delays in getting insurance approvals for the procedure if discharged. He did not press me to decide right then, but to let my nurse know my decision.

After conferring with my husband, my daughter, Faith, a registered nurse, and my son, Reginald, we agreed that I should go home and return later. I still had so much to do to prepare for our upcoming activities, which would allow me a few extra days to make any last-minute preparations. Besides, I didn't want to feel rushed into an invasive procedure by a physician who appeared hurried without having some understanding about the procedure and potential contraindications, as I would not be seeking a second opinion. When you know God's voice, you don't need another's opinion on a matter concerning yourself. Up until that point, no one had mentioned the term "cancer."

On that July 3rd, my valley walk began, involving several hospitalizations and numerous invasive tests, commencing with the stent placement on the 10th to open the bile duct to alleviate the obstruction and access tissue samples of the mass causing the blockage. This procedure was followed by a couple of MRIs (one of which I aborted due to anxiety), and another endoscopic ultrasound and biopsy, none of which provided conclusive results. What was clear after several weeks, amidst the uncertainty of a definitive diagnosis, was the ominous growth of the tumor mass, causing escalating pain levels, and unfavorable lab results. Struggling with the intensifying pain with every step I took and every meal I consumed, I tearfully informed my gastroenterologist that I could no longer endure *it*—whatever *it* was! Consequently, I was readmitted on October 10th, three months after the stent placement, for further evaluation concerning gallstones and consultation with a general surgeon.

While being wheeled to my hospital room in preparation for a newly ordered PET scan, I picked up a copy of *"The Daily Bread,"* a devotional booklet distributed in many hospitals, nursing homes, and confinement facilities. I love devotionals and short stories. After settling in, I opened it, and my gaze fell on the first day's title, "STOP!" I laid the booklet down momentarily as I contemplated my next, this new path, whatever it may be. I picked the guide up later to read the remaining portion of the devotional, "STOP!" The accompanying scripture was from Psalm chapter 46 and verse 10 in the New International Versions echoed deeply: *"He says, 'Be still, and know that I am God; I will be exalted among the nations, I will be exalted in the earth.'"* I firmly believe that God communicates with us through various mediums, like people, places, even books, and He just spoke to me. There's more to my life story!

That message felt tailor-made for me. It was as if God sent me an email urging me to embrace stillness, quiet all thoughts of uncertainty, and trust His ever present guidance. In that moment, I found reassurance that God's perfect will would illuminate not just my path but also that of the doctors, and all those I encountered by sharing my testimony. My source of peace remained grounded in the scriptures, a steadfast anchor in turbulent times. Remember Job?

After absolutely ruling out gallstones, the general surgeon recommended another endoscopic ultrasound and a second PET scan, because the first technician didn't follow the specific protocols. This time, the ultrasound and PET scans both showed a hypoechoic lesion on the head of my pancreas, raising suspicions of an absolute malignancy. Additionally, a chest CT scan unveiled a new right upper lung nodule. Subsequently, the general surgeon referred me to a surgical oncologist, who had discussed my case with a tumor board for assessment and recommendations prior to seeing me.

It was a beautiful Sunday morning on October 15th, 2023 . I had participated in my community's online morning devotional hour, had breakfast, and was resting when Dr. Joshua Shaw, the surgical oncologist, entered my room. After congenitally introducing himself, *I knew*. I had previously researched my symptoms and just needed confirmation. Dr. Shaw's solemn facial expression aided me in releasing the question I harbored for months, which I finally gave voice to— "*Is it cancer?*" He nodded affirmatively, adding that the mass was in the area of the head of my pancreas. Talk about timing, at that moment my husband, who was en route to Sunday service, telephoned to check in on me. I placed our phone conversation in speaker mode, facilitating introductions between my husband and the doctor. Dr. Shaw went on to elaborate on the challenges of diagnosing pancreatic cancer and expounded on the necessity of numerous tests for a more definitive diagnosis. He further elaborated that the last PET scan indicated a definitive uptake. Fortunately, the cancer had not metastasized beyond the area of the head of the pancreas.

When I asked for his recommended course of treatment, he proposed the overly complex *Whipple* surgery. Dr. Shaw began to describe the details of the procedure, but from the outset it was too intense, so I prompted him to halt his explanation and gave him this response, *"My husband and I are not afraid of cancer, and we're not afraid of death!"* Expressing our faith and confidence in divine intervention, I assured Dr. Shaw of our intentions to seek guidance from the realms of Heaven (through prayer) while he deliberated my case with the tumor board. My response to our lack of fear of cancer or death, and our invoking God's guidance during this critical juncture made an impression on Dr. Shaw. I was firmly assured that Dr. Shaw was assigned to my case by Divine Providence. Subsequently, on this eventful day, I was discharged, ready to embark on the next phase of this unforeseen journey. Later, I was told I was "his favorite patient" by my Nurse Navigator, Corinne.

A few days after arriving home, I said to my husband, *"I cannot locate fear."* That Inner Voice responded, *"Because I have not given you the spirit of fear!"* While many associate the word "cancer" with dread and death, my initial response departed from the norm. Confident in God's sovereignty, my case was in God's hands. Whatever the outcome, it would align with His Divine plan, and we would find contentment in His will.

In the weeks leading up to my surgery scheduled for November 16th, I had several intense moments grappling with disbelief that I had cancer. I shared the news with my children, church family, and a selective group of friends and associates, individuals whose prayers I valued. Rather than making a social media announcement that might invite numerous questions and opinions, I maintained my focus on hearing God's voice alone. As I often say, second opinions are needless when you discern God's guidance.

As I shared my plight, many individuals shared stories of their loved ones and acquaintances who succumbed to pancreatic cancer, mainly due to late-stage diagnoses. The gravity of such narratives weighed heavily, underscoring the potential severity of my situation. However weighty their experiences were, that distinct initial directive lingered in my mind—*"Go to Holy Cross Hospital!"* I kept reminding myself that God has a plan for my life and that this valley experience is not solely about me. *"Be still and know that I am God!"*

Delving into research on pancreatic cancer, a previously unfamiliar territory, I unraveled sobering statistics. Pancreatic cancer is renowned for its lethality, often diagnosed in advanced stages where surgical intervention may no longer be viable. While its prevalence is higher in the African American community, it affects all ages, genders, and ethnic groups. Not easily diagnosed, when it is, the mortality rates decline. When I conferred with my insurance carrier, even their mortality tables reiterated the grim outcome of such a diagnosis.

I further learned a harsh reality—a mere 20% of pancreatic cancer patients qualify for the Whipple procedure (I am grateful to be in that 20%). While the median life expectancy post-procedure stands at five years, many survivors have surpassed this prognosis, tenaciously embracing normalcy once more. I grappled with all this information when Holy Spirit gave me another directive - *"Stop the research and go through the process!"*

Oh, but God! His intervention on my behalf manifested in the containment of my tumor mass, which expanded from 2.2 to 3.2 centimeters between diagnosis and surgical intervention. The post-surgical tissue samples, however, revealed the presence of two metastatic hepatic lymph nodes among the 16 tested, alongside a definitive diagnosis of pancreatic adenocarcinoma. A rigorous chemotherapy regimen became imperative.

Following the Whipple procedure that took place on November 16th, one month later, I began the prescribed 12 biweekly chemotherapy infusions, which entailed 42 hours of steady infusions per round. The relentless challenges post-surgery (feeding tubes, elimination issues due to the restructuring of my digestive tract, and postoperative pain) coupled with the grueling side effects of chemotherapy--extreme fatigue, nausea, loss of appetite, neuropathy, and emotional isolation, I wanted to cry, but I was too weak to do even that. There were times I wanted to give up, but that was not an option. And I DID NOT want to die because I had too much left to do and a whole of love to give.

After the 6th round of chemo on March 6, 2024, I had become so weak and sickly that I grappled with the continuation of the infusions. I eventually told my husband of my decision to refuse the next treatment. He supported whatever decision I made. But on our way to the infusion center on March 20th for my scheduled visit with my oncologist and the next "fix," which I had planned to decline, as we were turning onto the Interstate, I heard the Lord say, *"Finish the process."* I told my husband and we both agreed with God. By His grace, He strengthened me to conclude His prescribed treatment regimen. Little did I know, He had already decided that I would have no more infusions after only six rounds. It was on that day that Dr. Nagovski "paused" all chemo infusions, but followed me for the next three months. I would have to go on a regimen to rebuild my white blood cells, which had become dangerously low. Hallelujah, I finished *"the process!"*

All DNA tests that were taken monthly from January of 2024 to now have negated any lingering cancer cells within my system. The chemo port was removed on July 2nd, 2024, marking a significant milestone. And the celebratory ringing of the "cancer free" bell on July 8th at the Michael and Dianne Bienes Comprehensive Cancer Center in Fort

Lauderdale, Florida, epitomized my triumph over adversity—an emotional testament to emerging cancer-free. Indeed, I walked THROUGH the valley.

This unforgettable encounter with cancer thrust me into one such valley of death, testing my faith and fortitude in ways I never could have imagined. Yet, precisely in this crucible of adversity, I came to understand more deeply what it means to live in *"the spirit of the Gospel."* The spirit of the Gospel, epitomized in the life and teachings of Jesus Christ, is a spirit of unwavering faith amidst uncertainty, boundless hope amidst despair, and unconditional love amidst suffering. During my battle with cancer, the Gospel's message became a luminous compass, guiding me through the darkest of times and bringing clarity to the chaos.

Faith, at its core, calls us to trust in the unseen and believe in the promises of God, even when circumstances seem bleak. In my valley, I learned to lean not on my understanding but trust in God's excellent plan. *"Be still, and know that I am God,"* the scripture beckoned, reminding me that I could find peace in His sovereignty by surrendering my worries and fears.

Hope, one of the greatest gifts of the Gospel, became my anchor. It was hope that sustained me through countless tests, treatments, and moments of despair. It reminded me that the valley is not the end, it's merely a passage. And there's always dawn after the darkest night. The Gospel teaches us that with every cross, there is a death and a resurrection – a triumph over adversity. I died to hopelessness, but I've risen to new life and possibilities.

Love, the essence of the Gospel, was found in the compassionate acts of those around me. From the medical staff who attended to me with kindness, my family, friends, and church community who showered me with prayers and encouragement, I experienced a profound sense of being enveloped in God's love. This love not only bolstered my spirit but became a source of strength I share with others, reinforcing the interconnectedness of our human experience.

Reflecting on my journey, I see how *"the spirit of the Gospel"* provided a framework for enduring and overcoming my trials. It taught me that we are never alone. Even in the deepest valleys, God walks with us, guides us, and uses our experiences to reveal His glory and purposes. In sharing this patch in my quilt of life, I hope to inspire you to embrace the spirit of the Gospel in your own life. Whether you are facing cancer or any other trial, may you find faith in God's promises, hope in His salvation, and love in His presence. Let the elements of faith, hope, and love illuminate your path as you walk through your valley. As your life's quilt is woven together with patches of valley and mountain experiences, you, too, can find solace in the knowledge that every trial, hardship, and challenge you face is an adventure towards more significant growth, deeper understanding, and profound tenacity.

I pray that my journey stands as a lighthouse of hope and a reminder that even in the depths of the valley and shadows of death, there exists a path to renewal, transformation, and triumph. I call it God's grace! As you are reading this chapter, you, or someone you love is walking or will walk through the arduous journey of cancer. It's a path marked by unique challenges and moments that test one's strength to its very core. I discovered that amidst the trial, the human spirit can harness incredible resilience, and just a few words of support can make a significant difference in our daily lives. I hope my story has reached deep into your heart, lifted your spirits, and given you a light for your path through the valley, with encouragement to carry you forward. I pray you will find solace in knowing others understand your struggle and are rooting for your victory. Courage resides within you, even when it feels out of reach.

My heart abounds with empathy for fellow warriors battling cancer or any terminal illness. Witnessing the anguish etched on the faces of my fellow infusion center comrades stirred profound compassion within me. Prompted by a desire to share the peace and joy amidst the battle wounds experienced through my suffering, I penned *"31 Days of Encouragement, Inspiration, and Affirmation for Cancer Warriors,"* a devotional booklet sponsored for distribution among warriors at infusion centers worldwide. Now driven by a deeper sense of purpose, I aim to extend my narrative beyond mere survival, aspiring to inspire and uplift those weathering their personal valley experiences.

Let me also affirm your journey and your feelings. Life's path often leads us through valleys—those lowly and usually lonely places where shadows loom large and challenges seem insurmountable. Journeying through the grips of cancer became a stark reminder of how these valleys can test our resolve, challenge our spirit, and unveil our deepest wells of strength and toughness. Each step taken in faith, each moment of doubt bravely faced, each flicker of hope kindled in the darkness became a testament to *"I can do all things through Christ who strengthens me"* (Philippians 4:13). I discovered that even in the darkest valleys, there exists a wellspring of light—a light that shines brightest when hope seems dimmest. With unwavering faith, resolve, and steadfast courage, I weathered the storms, emerged more robustly, and embraced perseverance's transformative power; and so can you.

My Unforgettable is a testament to the enduring power of the human spirit, capable of transcending even the most profound valleys life may lead us through. Within these valleys, we uncover hidden strengths, discover or rediscover our faith, and forge an unwavering determination to emerge victorious against all odds.

Psalm 23 for Cancer Warriors by Helen M. Gaines

The Lord is my shepherd, even when faced with cancer;
I have all that I need to guide me through the process.
He lets me rest in the green meadows of His Sovereignty,
He leads me beside peaceful waters of His love and grace.
He restores my weary soul through the promises of His Word.

Even when I walk through the dark valley of cancer,
I will not be afraid, for You are close beside me.
Your rod of protection and Your staff of comfort provide solace.
You prepare a feast for me in the presence of my fears.
You honor me by anointing my head with oil;
My cup overflows with Your blessings.

Surely Your goodness and unfailing love will pursue and overtake me
All the days of my life, and I will live in Your Presence, *forever*!

Ciara Lewis

Owner of KLConsulting LLC

https://www.linkedin.com/in/ciara-l-51bbbb204/
https://www.facebook.com/KLConsultingLLC/
https://www.instagram.com/klconsultingllc
https://klconsultllc.com/

Ciara Lewis, born and raised in Kentucky, started writing poetry at the age of 12. She won her first poetry award in Middle School from an original poem she wrote for her grandma titled "Watching Over Me." This was just the beginning of her journey in poetry.

Ciara has a background in Medical Information Technology and Medical Billing/Coding. Ciara is the owner of KLConsulting LLC, a Medical Billing and Credentialing Business. Although her background is in Medical Billing, Ciara has always loved helping people through her poetry.

Ciara will not only produce poetry books, but will in the near future put poetry on blankets, mugs and more. She is going to be a guiding light for those who are interested in growing as a poet. Connect with Ciara via email at cecespoetrycorner@gmail.com

My Little Miracle

By Ciara Lewis

To my #1 supporter, Yahuah, for loving me unconditionally, walking with me, allowing me to write this book, providing the wonderful people who have supported me, and most of all, allowing me to become a mother to my baby girl.

To my beautiful baby girl who has given me hope and inspiration. You have allowed me to see life's true meaning and pushed me beyond limits I never could have imagined.

To my sweet grandmother, Carolyn E Jones, for always looking out for me and listening to me. You were my rock and my foundation. (May your soul rest in peace)

To my wonderful mother, who has given me the best gift of life and understanding, thank you for being my anchor and best friend and never giving up on me. You have always been my sunshine through every storm.

To my special friend Myron J. Satterfield, thank you for being there for me in a time of need and helping me find my direction again. Thank you for understanding and supporting me during this most important time in my life. Thank you for giving me a safe place to stay and the support needed to help me prepare to bring my daughter into this world.

To the Bowman/Satterfield family, thank you for your hospitality and for helping me get to all of my appointments, protecting me, and ensuring I had all I needed to prepare for the birth of my child. I will never be able to thank you enough for all you did. A special thank you to Myron J Satterfield's mother for being a huge support, giving me the valuable talk about life and becoming a mother, but better yet, giving me the courage to know that I could still be a good mother even at a young age.

I love you all from the bottom of my heart. I wouldn't have been able to write this book without you all.

We always think we have our lives planned out until the unexpected happens. We then must decide how to play out the scenario and whether we will let it positively or negatively affect our lives. I was 17 and in high school, working at Goody's and playing volleyball, before the Yahuah changed my life forever. I had no clue how much and how quickly my life would change. I realized I had missed my period for April and started to get a little concerned, so I took a pregnancy test to be safe. It came back negative, so I waited a bit longer to see if it would show up, but there was still nothing. My mom then started asking about it and had me take another pregnancy test. That test was also negative, so we made an appointment with Dr.Johnson for a second opinion. I had issues before with my period being late, so we thought there was something medically wrong at first. The doctor ran some tests and felt around my stomach. He told me he believed it was a gastro problem and sent me some medicine to the pharmacy and a referral to a gastro. He had also run a blood pregnancy test and told us that he would call us in a few days with the results. I had gone back to playing volleyball and hanging out with my friends, not realizing anything was wrong. I felt fine.

About a week later, he called back with the results and said that I was pregnant and was about 3 to 5 months. I told my mom that couldn't be correct. If I were pregnant, I would have had to have been further along than that. We decided to drive to another small town about 45 minutes from home to get a second opinion and confirm exactly how far along I was. We get to the doctor, who tells us they want to do an ultrasound, which should give us further answers. They call us back, and I'm lying on the table, a nervous wreck but excited at the same time because I'm going to get to see my baby and hear the heartbeat for the first time. The lady starts putting the gel on me and moving the device around but then gets this concerned look. As she moved it, I noticed we couldn't hear the heartbeat, so I started to get nervous. She told me to relax and that sometimes this could happen if the baby has moved to a funny position. She repositioned the device, and finally, we started to hear the heartbeat. She then says to me, it looks like you're about eight months pregnant. My mouth almost hit the floor, and I looked at my mom in shock. It all made sense. I knew there was no way I could have only been 3 to 5 months. She told me my daughter was already positioned down and about ready to come out.

On the drive back home, my mom and I talked about what to do and how we would move forward. My mom knew I had always been very mature for my age and had an old soul. I had already said I most definitely wasn't having an abortion, but I also knew I still had to finish school and had a future to think about. I didn't have much time to think, so I went home and started Praying and thinking about my situation. I was supposed to go and stay with a friend that summer in a town about two hours from home where I wanted to go to college. I knew I couldn't go there anymore with my situation and put that burden on her and her family. I was on the phone with another friend living in the same area, telling him the situation while talking. He offered to let me come and stay at his house, and he would help me with my appointments until I figured out what I wanted to do. I discussed this with my mom, who said if I wanted to do it and felt comfortable, she would support me. I didn't want to have my baby in my hometown because the hospital had a bad reputation, and I didn't want to take any chances. I also needed somewhere quiet to think and focus on what I wanted to do and make the right decision. Let's say the

Yahuah knew exactly what he was doing and where he sent me. He guided me and protected me the whole way.

I left the weekend school let out for the summer and drove two hours to my friend's house. He greeted me once I got there and helped me get settled in. At the time, I still didn't look pregnant and was still wearing regular clothes; he kept asking me if I was sure I was pregnant. We talked the next day at his house, and he asked me if I had a plan yet. I was still scared and unsure of what I was doing then, but I felt I was in the right place. I told him I was going to look into adoption and the options for it. I just couldn't come to terms with not being a part of my child's life, better yet not ever knowing my child at all. I struggled for a while with this. He helped me find an adoption agency, and I scheduled an appointment to meet with her and a few families at the mall that weekend. I had the choice of still being a part of my baby's life to where the parents would allow me to make contact on her birthday and holidays, or some would even allow you to visit after a certain point. I met with three families, all of whom were wonderful and sweet. I picked out one family who seemed like it would have been a good life for her due to their background and having two other kids. However, I still just wasn't 100% settled with the decision. The way my adoption was going to be set up was I was going to be able to see and hold my baby and decide if I still wanted to go through with it or not, and the parents would have been on standby. The adoption lady told me that she was there to support me for anything I needed up until the birth of my child. She told me to call her anytime and that she would even come to the hospital with me when it was time for delivery.

Later that day, I returned to the house and was torn on what to do. My friend came in and told me that he had talked to his mom, and she wanted to talk with me. I knew then I was in trouble, but I knew this was my Guardian Angels protecting me and my child. His mom came over and had me come into the living room so she could talk to me.

She gave me a good long talk about life, a woman's responsibility, being a mother, and telling me that once I give my child to someone else, I will never be able to undo that or get her back. She told me that once I hold her, I will never want to let her go, and the first thing I will want to do is protect her from anything and everything. She let me know that I was carrying another life inside me, and although it may not have seemed real right then because she wasn't physically in my arms, it was just as real as if she were. She told me that if I ever needed anything, she would help me. I fell in love with his mom from that moment on. She gave me a gift that day that no one else can ever give me or take away. She saved my life and allowed me to see the bigger picture and realize that, yes, I made the adult decision to have my child, and now it was time for me to make the adult decision to raise my child and that I could do it. She also told me my mother would love me either way and would support me. She said, "Your mother will love this baby just as much as you, if not more." I couldn't thank her enough for what she did for me and the rest of the family.

I had found my second family from my friend helping me. He had two other Brothers who would come around and a few close family friends. They all looked out for me, helped me with my appointments, and ensured I had everything. The younger brother also lived in the house, and at first, he wasn't very fond of me, so he didn't say a lot initially, but eventually, he started to warm up to me. One day, my friend came to me and told me he had to leave for a while and take care of some business, but he would be back in a few weeks. He told me his brother and family would ensure I had everything I needed and got to and from my appointments. He also left me some money to ensure I was okay while he was gone. I was reticent and shy and didn't say much until I got comfortable. His brother came home one day and asked me if I had eaten, and I said no. He said, "Come on, we are going to the store." I was shocked because that was the first time he had talked to me. We conversed on the way to the store and got to know each other. We found that we had quite a few things in common and thought a lot alike. He told me that he knew it had to be rough what I was going through, but he knew I would be a good mother, and I could do it. He told me I could let him know anytime I needed something or if I needed to go somewhere. From that day forward, he promised to try to stay home more so I wasn't there alone, and if he wasn't home and I needed something, to call him.

From that point forward, he became a brother figure to me, and his mom became a mother figure. She would come to get me out of the house, take me to eat, go shopping, and talk to me. He would come home from work, check in on me, and ensure I had eaten or didn't need anything. He would then leave for a while, return at night, and ensure I was still doing okay. My friend would call and check-in. I was getting close to my due date at this point, and I was starting to show. I was about two weeks from delivering my daughter. One day, I began not to feel so well, and he had to take me to the hospital. Something was going on with my blood pressure and my daughter's heart rate. They had to put me on a machine and keep me overnight to monitor us. I was nervous, but we finally got everything leveled back out. The doctor told me that I needed to start walking and that it would help push the delivery along. My mom came up to see me that weekend and took me out to eat and for a long walk across the bridge downtown. The next night, I went into labor, and I was home by myself. His brother had asked me if I needed him to stay home or if I was ok. I told him I was fine, and I could call if I needed anything; little did I know I was going to go into labor. I didn't think I was in labor, but I was on the phone with my mom, and I kept feeling funny. I tried to get up and walk but could barely do so. My mom said oh my gosh, you're in labor. I knew I had to get to the hospital, and I wasn't about to call the ambulance because the hospital was right down the street. I got in the car and drove down to the hospital. When I got there, I told them I needed labor and delivery. They thought I was playing a prank on them because I didn't look pregnant, and at one point, the lady threatened to call the police on me because she thought I was joking. I told her if she didn't get me a wheelchair right now, I was going to have my baby on the floor. She immediately got a wheelchair and wheeled me upstairs; as soon as the nurse got me in the bed, my water broke.

I called my mom, the adoption lady, and texted my friend and his brother once I settled in. The adoption lady offered to come and sit with me until my mom arrived. By the time the adoption lady got there, they had started me on pain medicine and were getting ready to do my epidural. She held my hand and sat with me until my mom arrived. I had a complicated delivery. I remember them showing me my daughter, but they wouldn't let me hold her, and I started crying. I also remember the doctor being down there a long time, but he kept trying to talk to me and keep my focus off everything. He told me I had a significant tear, and he had to give me some special stitching. They finally sent me to a room, and I finally got to see my mom. I was so out of it and couldn't feel anything from the waist down. The next day, the nurse came in, and I still couldn't feel anything, but they kept telling me that it should have worn off by now. I needed to go to the restroom, and the nurse refused to help; she kept telling me I could do it myself. I tried to get up and almost fell, going to the bathroom. That got her attention quickly. She finally said, "That's odd; you should be able to feel and walk by now." I'll let the doctor know you're still having trouble. They kept us for a few days to be safe before letting us go home. His brother came up to see the baby before we got released, and I took her to his mom's house before we headed back to my hometown. A part of me didn't want to leave because I had gotten so used to being there with them, but I knew I had to get back home to my life and raise my daughter. Either way, I knew from that point forward I had a new family in my corner who had forever helped change my life.

By the time we got home, I wasn't feeling well and knew something was off. My aunt and her kids were at my grandma's, where we also lived. My aunt offered to take me to the hospital because she knew something wasn't right as well. We got to the hospital, and they got me back and started running some tests. They first tried to return and tell us it was a UTI before the X-ray. I knew it had to be more than a UTI because I had never had one make me feel like that. They took me back for my X-ray, and they asked me whether I had any metal on me, and I said no. They took the first set of pictures, and the lady returned with a concerned look and said, "Are you sure you don't have any metal on you? I said no, and she came, patted me down, and said, mmm. Ok, let me try it again. She takes the second picture and returns with a concerned look. She says there are no piercings or anything. I said no. She took one last set of images and came around and said, I don't know how to tell you this, but you have a piece of metal in your body. I was in complete shock and didn't know what to say. The ER doctor returns and says it should pass through your system. I thought there was no way a piece of metal that size would bypass. I'm also thinking oh my gosh, they just left metal in me from having my daughter.

We got back home and told my mom and grandma what they had said, and they were shocked. I had an appointment to see a general surgeon, and they wanted to go in blind and take it out. At this point, months go by, and I'm not getting any better, only sicker. They kept running tests and figuring out how to take it out. I told them I wanted a second opinion, and they sent me to UK. The Doctor there came up with a good game plan and said we will go in laparoscopically and take it out. It should be an in-and-out surgery. By the time I had my surgery, it was in January 2008. The day of my surgery, I had freaked out and was trying to get out of it. The doctor came in, sat down on my bed, held my hand, looked at me, and said, if you don't have this surgery today, you will die within the next week, if not less. He told me that the metal had started to eat around my small bowel and large intestines and was causing a severe infection. He said the doctors should have taken the metal out months before that. He promised he was going to take good care of me and do his best to keep me alive. He saved my life that day, but he did end up having to take a large portion of my large intestines. I have been sick ever since and am now diagnosed with Crohn's disease.

After the surgery, my life changed forever: constant doctor appointments, procedures, infections, etc. I have been sick ever since that day. To this day, we still don't have an accurate diagnosis or a way to fix it. I can now barely eat, I have had to change my diet drastically, I am constantly in pain, I don't feel well, and I have several doctor appointments. However, I went back to high school on homebound and graduated. The school dean tried to stop me from walking on stage and getting my letterman jacket because I had to do my work at home. I told her it wasn't fair because I was still doing my schoolwork just like everyone else and passing with a 4.0 GPA. My teachers also helped me fight to have the privilege to walk across the stage, to accept my diploma, and to get my letterman jacket. After having my daughter, I graduated with my class of 2008 after several people thought I wouldn't finish high school. Not only did I finish high school with a 4.0 GPA, raised my daughter, almost died twice, and went through an abusive relationship. I even went to college and got my degree in Medical Information Technology and a career in Medical Billing and Coding.

My daughter is now 16 and turning 17 on July 18, and I couldn't be a prouder mother. She is a straight-A student and has a good, strong head on her shoulders. She has a life plan and works hard every day. My daughter has been my inspiration since birth, and she will never know how much I need her. She is my strength and what keeps me going.

I started my own Medical Billing and Credentialing Business (named after my daughter KLConsulting LLC) 4 years ago and just graduated from the One Million Women's Black in Business program through Goldman Sachs. It's funny how the Yahuah works and reconnects people. We moved back to the town where my daughter was born and where my friend and his family still live. We have all reconnected, and it has been a blessing to get back to my second family and see how everyone has grown.

We should never judge a book by its cover or give up on someone because their situation may not make sense to us or may seem like they can't finish the race. The truth is that when Yahuah is working for his children, we never know what that person can accomplish. I'm sure it is easy for some people to think that if someone has a baby young, they may not be able to finish school or have a good life. Why would people think that? Because that's the way the world has taught us how to think and view situations. I hope to be an inspiration to others and let them know that it is possible. I was very BLESSED to be able to have my daughter finish school, go through the traumatic medical issues that came along with it and the abusive relationship, and still somehow come out doing pretty well for myself. Not only that, but I was also able to give my daughter a good life. Sure, maybe someone else was more prosperous than me or had more than me, but could they have been able to give her the same love and value as her mother? His mom always left me with that question and had me think about it daily. It has been challenging, but I think being a mother is the most challenging job in the world. You're 100% responsible for another human's life inside you and when they are born for up to 18 years after. It still doesn't stop then, either. You literally hold someone else's life and future in your own hands.

Me and My Babygirl Kiara

JOIN THE MOVEMENT!
#BAUW

Becoming An Unstoppable Woman
With She Rises Studios

She Rises Studios was founded by Hanna Olivas and Adriana Luna Carlos, the mother-daughter duo, in mid-2020 as they saw a need to help empower women worldwide. They are the podcast hosts of the *She Rises Studios Podcast* and Amazon best-selling authors and motivational speakers who travel the world. Hanna and Adriana are the movement creators of #BAUW - Becoming An Unstoppable Woman: The movement has been created to universally impact women of all ages, at whatever stage of life, to overcome insecurities, and adversities, and develop an unstoppable mindset. She Rises Studios educates, celebrates, and empowers women globally.

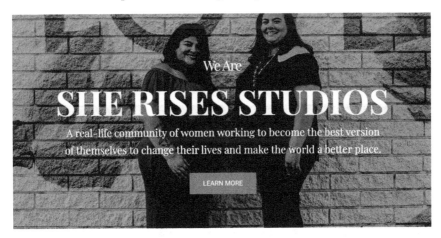

Looking to Join Us in our Next Anthology or Publish YOUR Own?

She Rises Studios Publishing offers full-service publishing, marketing, book tour, and campaign services. For more information, contact info@sherisesstudios.com

We are always looking for women who want to share their stories and expertise and feature their businesses on our podcasts, in our books, and in our magazines.

SEE WHAT WE DO

OUR PODCAST   OUR BOOKS   OUR SERVICES

Be featured in the Becoming An Unstoppable Woman magazine, published in 13 countries and sold in all major retailers. Get the visibility you need to LEVEL UP in your business!

Have your own TV show streamed across major platforms like Roku TV, Amazon Fire Stick, Apple TV and more!

Learn to leverage your expertise. Build your online presence and grow your audience with FENIX TV.
https://fenixtv.sherisesstudios.com/

Visit www.SheRisesStudios.com to see how YOU can join the #BAUW movement and help your community to achieve the UNSTOPPABLE mindset.

Have you checked out the *She Rises Studios Podcast?*

Find us on all MAJOR platforms: Spotify, IHeartRadio, Apple Podcasts, Google Podcasts, etc.

Looking to become a sponsor or build a partnership?

Email us at info@sherisesstudios.com

Made in the USA
Middletown, DE
16 May 2025

75592979R10106